Assessment as Inquiry

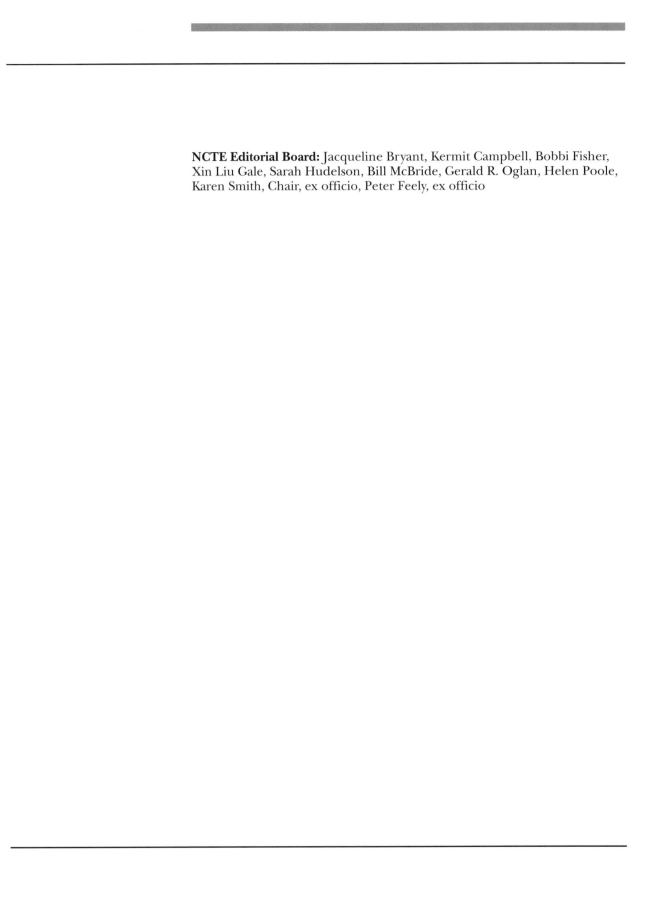

Assessment as Inquiry

Learning the Hypothesis-Test Process

Edited by

Diane Stephens
University of Hawaii at Manoa
Honolulu, Hawaii

Jennifer Story
Dole Middle School
Honolulu, Hawaii

National Council of Teachers of English
1111 W. Kenyon Road, Urbana, Illinois 61801-1096

Manuscript Editor: Michelle Sanden Johlas

Interior Design: Doug Burnett

Cover Design: Pat Mayer

NCTE Stock Number: 27851-3050

Library of Congress Cataloging-in-Publication Data

Assessment as inquiry: learning the hypothesis-test process/edited by
Diane Stephens, Jennifer Story.
      p. cm.
    Includes bibliographical references (p.).
    ISBN 0-8141-2785-1 (pbk. : alk. paper)
    1. Educational tests and measurements. 2. Teacher-student
relationships—Case studies. 3. Reading (Elementary) I. Stephens, Diane.
II. Story, Jennifer.

LB3051.A76665 1999
371.27'2—dc21

                                               99-047462

This book was typeset in New Baskerville and Optima by Electronic Imaging.
Typefaces used on the cover were Universe Condensed and Benquiat Gothic Book.
The book was printed by Versa Press.

Contents

Editors' Note: For our readers' convenience, the Hypothesis-Test sheets (as well as the miscue analysis sheets) shown in this book have been typeset from the originals. Since HT is a process with many cycles, the teachers' originals, usually handwritten, were (as you might guess) covered with sticky-notes, arrows, cross-outs, misspellings, shorthand. We felt it more important to convey the substance (rather than original form) of the HT process, as shown by the teachers' observations, interpretations, hypotheses, and curricular decisions.

1 What Is the Hypothesis-Test Process?

Introduction

Diane Stephens,
with **Jennifer Story, Kitty Aihara, Stephanie Hisatake, Bette Ito, Carrie Kawamoto, Sandie Kubota, Jocelyn Mokulehua, Susan Oka-Yamashita, Sarah Omalza, Elaine Tsuchiyama, Frances Yamate, Lynn Yoshizaki,** and **Diane Yoshizawa**

Explains the genesis of the HT process and provides an overview of this book.

Several years ago, in an article in *Language Arts,* Mem Fox (1988) used the expression "ache with caring" (p. 113). I've used that expression several times since to describe myself. For me, the ache shows up in lots of places, but it has always been a part of my relationship to people who don't feel successful as readers. I can trace that ache back to my first teaching job, and I can follow it through all the jobs I have held since. With the ache—the wanting to help—has come worry: Will I be *able* to help?

Eventually, with the help of a lot of the people I worked with and the people whose work I read (most notably, Yetta Goodman [1985] on kidwatching, and Piaget, in Ginsberg and Opper [1979] on observing and asking questions), I was less worried about my ability to be helpful to people who struggled as readers, writers, learners. I began to believe I *could* help. This occurred just about the time I graduated from a doctoral program at Indiana University.

And then I was offered my first college-level teaching job. As part of that job, I was asked to teach a master's level course on reading assessment. I remember feeling as if the bottom had dropped out. I felt as if I didn't have a clue about what to do. I had just begun to worry a little less about my ability to be helpful. How could I possibly help someone else feel the same way? How could I "teach" reading assessment?

I think of teaching, like writing, as a "back burner" process. Things simmer, until one day you wake up with an idea about what you might do/write. And so it was that I came up with a plan for "teaching" reading assessment. Basically, I decided that on the first

---

This chapter was adapted from an article published by the authors under the title "When Assessment Is Inquiry," which appeared in *Language Arts* (1996), 17(3), 105–112. In this chapter, *I* refers to the first author, Diane Stephens.

day of the graduate class, I would make explicit to others what I thought my mind did when I was trying to understand someone else as a learner. What I thought I did was:

A. Notice,

B. Think broadly about what might be going on,

C. Look across all possibilities and make my best guess,

D. Figure out what I could do to test my hypotheses, and then

E. Start noticing again.

It seemed to me that I kept this up until I trusted my understandings enough to take action. Because the entire process was informed and shaped by the theories I held, for a while I wanted to put (B)—the thinking about, which would make theory explicit—before (A), the noticing. However, I subsequently came to understand that it is through reflection that we begin to make our theories explicit for ourselves and others; therefore, I kept the original order.

On paper, this process ended up looking like Figure 1. I made copies of that paper and took it to class. I can't remember what I said that first night, but what I say now is that this is a way of thinking I am suggesting you try on, to see for yourself whether or not it is helpful to you. I explain that I have known a number of teachers who have found this way of thinking helpful. I use the name teachers in that first graduate class gave it: HT, for "Hypothesis-Test." This name focuses on the key components of the process I introduced to them: Making informed <u>H</u>ypotheses and <u>T</u>esting them out through practice.

Teaching is, for the most part, a private act. What teachers, including professors, do in their classrooms is rarely seen by anyone. And so, since that first graduate class, teachers and I have been messing about with this HT process, and nobody besides us has known about what we were doing/thinking. Over the years, by trying things out and talking about and reflecting upon our actions, we learned a lot. We came to understand that in the process of trying to figure out how someone else thinks, you end up learning about how you think. Working with the HT framework helped us understand that we don't always know as much as we need to know about how children learn, and this served as a catalyst to our learning more. We also came to see that HT works outside the one-on-one assessment process it was originally designed to serve. We have used HT to better understand all sorts of things—ourselves, our spouses, teenagers, curriculum, principals, and whole classrooms of learners. As Sandie Kubota, a Title 1 teacher, explained:

> I began to notice how Lynn Yoshizaki and I would discuss the children in the classroom. We began to think like the HT process. We would look at what a student was doing, try to make some interpretations

Hypothesis-Test Sheet			
Name _____ Teacher _____		Date _____ Page _____ of _____	
Observations	Interpretations	Hypotheses	Curricular Decisions

Figure 1. Sample Hypothesis-Test sheet.

and then observe some more. This became a natural thing for us to do. It was a positive way of looking at children that complemented our philosophies. I found myself doing this not only with Lynn but with other teachers when we would see each other in the hallway and talk about an observation we had made. Pretty soon, I was transferring this process to my personal life, to my nine-year-old son, and to my husband . . .

As we have worked and learned together, we have come to understand that the HT process, which began as an assessment process, becomes a learning process. Elaine Yoshioka, a district resource teacher, named this process "inquiry" when she visited our classroom one time and subsequently wrote:

> As I observed each teacher working with a child and as I heard and participated in the dialogue that followed the evening's work with the children, I realized that the puzzlements and wonderings about the child became an inquiry for the teacher. And this inquiry drove the teacher to want to understand the child as fully as she could and to want to learn more about how children learn to read. I was so taken by the learning that was occurring for the teachers and for me, even though I was only an observer, that I decided to attend every session.

A few years ago, some educators from the mainland asked to observe us as we worked with children, using the HT process. Like Elaine, they were impressed with the process, and they asked us to write about what we were doing and thinking. We decided to accept that invitation in the hopes that what we wrote would be helpful to other teachers and the children they worry about. We wrote an article for *Language Arts* in 1996 and then put together an issue of *Primary Voices* in 1997. Educators who read those documents or attended our presentations (e.g., NCTE's 1993 Annual Convention) encouraged us to explain more about the HT process, and this book is one of two we offer in response to those requests. This first book focuses on *learning* the HT process. The second, which is in process, focuses on *teaching* HT.

In the next chapter of this book we explain the "nuts and bolts" of the HT process, while the other chapters show how that process played out for several very different children and their teachers. In the second section, "Learning HT One-on-One," Susan Oka-Yamashita, Lynn Yoshizaki, Elaine Tsuchiyama, and Diane Parker address this inquiry process as they explain about how they learned the HT process and what they learned about reading, learning, and children as a result of that engagement. In these chapters, we keep the focus on the child and on helping the reader understand the HT process itself. In the third section, "Learning *from* One-on-One: HT in the Classroom," Sandie Kubota, Bette Ito, and Paula Matsunaga explore this inquiry process as they share the lessons they have taken away from HT and show how what they learned impacted their classroom practices.

We most sincerely hope that in making public our journey, we may be helpful to you on yours.

References

Fox, M. (1988). Notes from the battlefield: Towards a theory of why people write. *Language Arts, 65*(2), 112–125.

Ginsberg, H., & Opper, S. (1979). *Piaget's theory of intellectual development.* New Jersey: Prentice-Hall.

Goodman, Y. (1985). Kidwatching: Observing children in the classroom. In A. Jagger & T. Smith-Burke (Eds.), *Observing the language learner.* Newark, DE: International Reading Association.

Kawamoto, C. (1997). Driven to read. *Primary Voices K–6, 5*(1), 24–34.

Kubota, S. (1997). Learning begins with letting go. *Primary Voices K–6, 5*(1), 24b.

Mokulehua, J. (1997). You can't begin at the end. *Primary Voices K–6, 5*(1), 24c.

Oka-Yamashita, S. (1997). Teachers have to be learners. *Primary Voices K–6, 5*(1), 24d.

Omalza, S., Aihara, K., & Stephens, D. (1997). Engaged in learning through the HT Process. *Primary Voices K–6, 5*(1), 4–17.

Stephens, D., Story, J., Aihara, K., Hisatake, S., Ito, B., Kawamoto, C., Kubota, S., Mokulehua, J., Oka-Yamashita, S., Omalza, S., Tsuchiyama, E., Yamate, F., Yoshizaki, L., & Yoshizawa, D. (1996). When assessment is inquiry. *Language Arts, 17*(3), 105–112.

Stephens, D., Story, J., & Meyer-Reimer, K. (Eds.). (1997). Assessment as inquiry [themed issue]. *Primary Voices K–6, 5*(1). Urbana, IL: National Council of Teachers of English.

Story, J. (1997). Finding students before they find me: HT in the classroom. *Primary Voices K–6, 5*(1), 35–39.

Tsuchiyama. E. (1997). Devin, alligators, jellyfish, and me. *Primary Voices K–6, 5*(1), 40–42.

Yamate, F. C. (1997). Learning from one-on-one helps everyone. *Primary Voices K–6, 5*(1), 24a.

Yoshizaki, L. (1997). Reflections. *Primary Voices K–6, 5*(1), 43–45.

Yoshizawa, D. (1997). Learning with Jaime. *Primary Voices K–6, 5*(1), 18–23.

Overview of the HT Process

Diane Stephens, Jennifer Story, Kitty Aihara, Stephanie Hisatake, Bette Ito, Carrie Kawamoto, Sandie Kubota, Jocelyn Mokulehua, Susan Oka-Yamashita, Sarah Omalza, Elaine Tsuchiyama, Frances Yamate, Lynn Yoshizaki, Diane Yoshizawa

Explains the HT process by showing how it played out for Virgie, a third-grade child who also is a second-language learner with a hearing loss.

The Hypothesis-Test process is just that—a process. A way of thinking. We've given it a form, but after a while, most teachers keep the process and make up their own form. That's because (we want to emphasize in neon lights), **HT is a process, a way of thinking.** As a way of thinking, it has four recursive parts: observations, interpretations, hypotheses, and curricular decisions. Each of these parts has its own column on the HT sheet (see Figure 1, page 5).

How We Use the HT Sheet
Observations

In the first column, we record things we have noticed about a student we are worried about as a reader or learner. Two things make this difficult: (1) It's hard to figure out what is worth noticing and recording; and (2) It's hard to write down what you see instead of what you think about what you see. Both of these things get easier with time. Relative to the first difficulty, what happens is that you learn—from doing and from collaborating with others—which kinds of observations start you on a path to understanding and which ones dead-end. The hardest part is trusting the process. With practice, patterns emerge and it becomes clear what will be generative and what will not.

Relative to the second difficulty: well, we also work on this together. If a colleague tells us what he or she saw (for example, "When David came into the room, he stayed right by the door, sort of hugging it, and when anyone came near, he started to cry") then we are able to think with that person about what might be going on for

This chapter was adapted from an article published by the authors, "When Assessment Is Inquiry," which appeared in *Language Arts* (1996), 17(3), 105–112.

David; we can talk about why he might have behaved that way. On the other hand, if a colleague tells us that "David is insecure," there really isn't anything for us to say. The HT process is about *understanding*. We can't generate possibilities if a judgment has already been made.

By talking with each other about these kinds of things, we have gotten better at writing down observations that lead to helping us understand the child as learner. These observations are the first step on our path to understanding.

The Hypothesis-Test sheet shown in Example 1 shows the observations one teacher, Stephanie Hisatake, made about Virgie. Because Stephanie recorded what she saw, we were able to brainstorm possible interpretations, to think with her about what those observations could mean. These observations then turned out to be generative ones.

Interpretations   Once we have a number of observations about a child we are trying to understand, we use column two to record our ideas about what the observations might mean. Stephanie and her study group, for example, came up with ten interpretations (see Example 1) as possible explanations for Stephanie's fourth observation about Virgie's miscues. These interpretations become stepping stones to the hypotheses we make.

As part of this process, we have found that it helps to brainstorm at least five possible interpretations for each observation. That pushes us past our tendency to make spontaneous decisions and helps us better understand the child and our theories and practices. Sally Omalza, a sixth-grade teacher, explains how this process helped her grow:

> The process of making five interpretations led me to question the way I was making decisions in the classroom. I realized that in my haste I was not giving children the benefit of a deeper look into their concerns. . . . Now all that has changed. It has been amazing to see how much all of us [teachers] grew when we opened our minds and hearts to multiple possibilities.

As we have worked by ourselves and with each other to generate five possible interpretations for each observation, we have sometimes found that we needed to know more about how children learn and, in particular, about how children learn to read and write. Kitty Aihara, a Title 1 teacher, described what happened to her:

> The HT process pushed me to inquire and reflect on my beliefs and practices and, more importantly, to focus on the student as learner. In my search to systematically observe and formulate five interpretations, I found that I did not have a strong knowledge base about reading. . . . My quest to explore the "particulars" of readings and to

find words to interpret observations drove me to collaborate with others and to read professional literature. In this process of reflecting, searching, and taking action, I increased my knowledge of reading and of the conditions under which we learn.

When we generate possible interpretations together, we begin to make our theories explicit to each other and to ourselves. Indeed, as soon as we start to ask what something *means*, we are having a conversation about values and about our theories. Someone suggests, for example, that maybe David (who hugged the door in the example earlier) may not be much of a risk taker. That leads us to talking about risk taking. Do we believe that risk taking is an essential part of learning? Who has written about that? Whom should we read? And what does all this mean for our teaching? If we decide that risk taking is an important characteristic, how do we set up classrooms that help children take risks? Are our classrooms set up that way now? If not, what would have to change? We also start asking ourselves about other children in our classrooms. Are there other students who are reluctant to take risks? If so, who are they and what have we done to help them? Officially, we are talking about one child. In practice, however, we are broadly exploring, debating, and reflecting on our theories and our practices. By learning how to help one child, we learn to help each other and the other children in our classrooms.

Hypotheses

Once we have brainstormed possible interpretations for each observation, we look across all of the interpretations to identify possible patterns. These possible patterns get written down as hypotheses (third column) to explore. They are sometimes listed as questions, sometimes as statements.

When we first started using the HT process, we tended to write down one hypothesis for each observation. This turned out to be counterproductive, since we most often simply picked the interpretation we liked best and put it in the hypothesis column. We found out that it was more useful to look across all the interpretations and come up with four or five possible explanations that we wanted to explore the next time we were with the child. As Example 1 (see pages 11–13) shows, Stephanie generated several hypotheses to explore about Virgie.

Curricular Decisions

Curricular decisions are plans we make that will enable us to test out our hypotheses. The goal is to better understand the child as learner. Very often, these plans (recorded in column four) include observing more, listening more, and spending more time with the child and texts. Stephanie, for example, decided to talk to Virgie and her mother about Virgie's hearing and about Virgie's experiences with

Hypothesis-Test Sheet

Name __Virgie__

Teacher __Stephanie Hisatake__

Date _____

Page __1__ of __3__

Observations	Interpretations (by Observation #)	Hypotheses	Curricular Decisions
1. When Virgie was seated to my left and was engaging in conversation with me, she responded four times to my remarks by positioning her head close to me at an angle with her left ear facing me and said, "Huh."	1a. Virgie may not have been paying attention to what I was saying and moved closer when she realized she needed to. 1b. Saying "huh" is a way for her to buy time because she didn't know how to respond to what I said. 1c. She said "huh" and turned her head because she did not hear what I said. 1d. Virgie may have trouble hearing unless she focuses her attention. 1e. Virgie may have trouble hearing out of her right ear.	1. Virgie may have difficulty hearing (thus explaining her head turning and possibly her apparently limited understanding of sound–symbol relationships). 2. Virgie may not have a solid understanding of English (thus explaining her saying "huh" and also her struggle with both reading and writing). 3. Virgie may not have had much experience with print (thus explaining her unfamiliarity with the words *author* and *illustrator* as well as her reading and writing strategies and skills). 4. Virgie may not understand that reading is a meaning-making process (thus explaining her uncorrected miscues). 5. Virgie may not use her world knowledge to make meaning from text. 6. Virgie may not be aware that she can self-monitor and self-correct in order to make meaning from print. 7. Virgie lacks confidence in herself as a reader and as a writer. 8. Virgie may not have developed the skills and strategies she needs to be successful as a reader and as a writer.	1. Talk to her mother and understand her perspective. In particular, find out about her background as a speaker, reader, and writer of English and about her hearing. 2. Talk to mother and teacher about Virgie as a reader. 3. Talk to her to understand how she is thinking when she reads and writes. 4. Observe her some more in situations that involve both reading and writing.
2. Prior to reading *The True Story of the Three Little Pigs* (Scieszka, 1989), I read the title and author and pointed out the author's name. Virgie asked "What's an author?" When I asked what an illustrator was, Virgie shrugged her shoulders and said, "I don't know."	2a. Virgie may not have had much experience with books. 2b. Virgie may not have heard the word *author* or *illustrator* before. 2c. Virgie may be trying to avoid reading and so asks questions that delay the reading experience. 2d. Virgie may not know what an author and/or illustrator is. 2e. Virgie may not understand how what one writes becomes a book.		
3. When I asked her to read *There's a Hippopotamus under My Bed* (Thaler, 1978) during a Shared Reading Experience, Virgie immediately picked up the book, opened it to the first page, and began to read aloud.	3a. Virgie understood the directions I gave her. 3b. Virgie responded to my directions by following them. 3c. Virgie understands that a book/story begins on the first page. 3d. Virgie seemed willing to take a risk and read as asked. 3e. Virgie understands that print is read from left to right and top to bottom.		

Example 1. Stephanie Hisatake's Hypothesis-Test sheet from her first one-on-one observations of Virgie, a nine-year-old third grader.

Example 1. Continued

Hypothesis-Test Sheet

Name _Virgie_

Teacher _Stephanie Hisatake_

Observations	Interpretations (by Observation #)	Hypotheses	Curricular Decisions
4. Virgie made numerous miscues on each page, often substituting nonsense words. She read quickly and the miscues were not corrected.	4a. Virgie may not understand what she is reading.		
	4b. Virgie may not be self-correcting when something does not make sense.		
	4c. Virgie may not know that she should self-correct.		
	4d. Virgie may not have a variety of strategies she can use to make meaning.		
	4e. Virgie may not perceive the task as meaningful.		
	4f. Virgie may not perceive the task as valuable.		
	4g. Virgie may not feel comfortable self-correcting.		
	4h. Virgie self-corrected silently but not orally.		
	4i. Virgie did not make connections between world knowledge and the text.		
	4j. Virgie did not have the world knowledge needed to make connections with the text.		
5. When I asked her to write her name, her sister's name, and their phone number, Virgie wrote legibly and without any hesitation.	5a. Virgie had memorized this information.		
	5b. Virgie perceived this task as meaningful.		
	5c. Virgie is willing to do a writing task when she is sure her response is correct.		
	5d. Virgie understands some of the conventions of print, e.g., that there are supposed to be spaces between words, that names start with a capital letter.		

Hypothesis-Test Sheet

Name   Virgie

Teacher   Stephanie Hisatake

Observations	Interpretations (by Observation #)	Hypotheses	Curricular Decisions
6. When I asked her to write in her journal about what had transpired that first day, Virgie shook her head and said, "No, I don't want to."	6a. Virgie is reluctant to take risks as a writer when she is not sure how to do the task. 6b. Virgie does not understand what I wanted her to do. 6c. Virgie understands but is afraid she can not do it. 6d. Virgie understands but is afraid she can not do it correctly. 6e. Virgie may have misunderstood (not heard) what the teacher asked. 6f. Virgie is embarrassed by her writing (spelling). 6g. Virgie may think words always have to be spelled conventionally.		
7. When I told her it would not be shared with others, she took the journal tablet and wrote, *I ran a dad and I rit my fnr.* She read her entry back to me, "I read a book and I write my sister's name and I write my sister's phone number."	7a. Virgie understands that there is a relationship between what is spoken and what is written. 7b. Virgie understands that what is written can be read. 7c. Virgie sometimes uses the strategy of "spelling as it sounds", e.g. /rit/ for *write*, /f/ for *ph* in *phone*. 7d. Virgie may not know the conventional spelling of many of the words she wrote. 7e. Virgie may not understand she is expected to use conventional spelling when she can. 7f. Virgie may not have seen very many words in print. 7g. Virgie may not have developed an extensive understanding of sound–symbol relationships. 7h. Virgie just wrote to get the task over with.		

Example 1. Continued

English and possibly with other languages. She talked to Virgie, her mother, and her teacher about Virgie as a reader. She tried to understand how much reading Virgie did and of what kinds of text. She recorded and analyzed miscues. She observed Virgie in a variety of reading situations to try to understand her confidence and her willingness to take risks. She talked to Virgie about what she was reading so she could better understand Virgie's meaning-making processes.

Initially, Stephanie jumped to "solutions" to try to fix what she almost instantaneously concluded were Virgie's problems. That first day, under curricular decisions, instead of designing ways to test out hypotheses, she proposed what we have come to call "quick fixes." Her quick fixes for Virgie included:

1. Provide a distraction-free environment.

2. Ask Virgie "Does that make sense?" when she does not self-monitor.

3. Model the use of semantic, syntactic, and grapho-phonemic cues.

Because we have learned over time that teachers first need to understand a child as reader/learner before being able to make informed decisions about how to be helpful, Stephanie realized she needed to back off from these "quick fixes" and instead focus on learning more about Virgie by using curricular decisions to test out her hypotheses.

Continuing the Process

Once curricular decisions have been made and carried out, we begin a new Hypothesis-Test cycle. On a new HT sheet, we record the observations we make while implementing our curricular decisions, consider new interpretations, make new hypotheses, and plan new curricular decisions. This recursive process continues for several cycles. Along the way, we start to become "pretty sure" about some of the patterns we are seeing. These "pretty sures" go on a cover sheet and are used to guide instruction.

Why We Bother

The HT process has evolved over a number of years, in North Carolina, Illinois, and Hawaii. I began using HT in graduate classes in North Carolina in 1986, subsequently moved to Illinois and used it there, and now use it in my graduate classes in Hawaii. In each of these communities, teachers have talked highly of the HT process and told stories about how it made a difference in their lives. Recently, a number of us here have been talking about why we value the HT process. We came up with three major reasons:

1. It provides time for us to be learners.

2. It provides time for students to be learners.

3. It focuses us on the particular, so we are able to make what Lynn Yoshizaki calls the "abstraction connection."

Time for Us to Be Learners

In traditional assessment, even in what is now being called "alternative assessment," the focus is on the child as learner and, in the best of worlds, the teacher expects to know more about the child as a result of the assessment. One category of people, students, is studied by another category of people, teachers.

When we use the HT process, however, what happens is that we as teachers become involved both in assessment of others and in assessment of ourselves. We start paying attention to how our minds work—to how we make connections, construct hypotheses, and draw conclusions. In making our thinking explicit and talking with others about how we are thinking, we raise our consciousness about the thinking/learning process. We think about our own thinking; we inquire into our own learning. In our self-examination, we name and reexamine our theories and, in turn, reconceptualize our practices. Susan Oka-Yamashita, for example, tells the story about how, in order to better understand the second grader she was working with, she started reading Frank Smith's *Understanding Reading* (1988). As she read, she paid attention to what she did as a reader. She realized that in the past she often was not able to make connections between what she was reading professionally and what she was doing as a teacher. This time, however, she did make connections. As she did so, "the text became easier, it began to make sense." She found herself reading because she "wanted to." This led her to wonder why things were different now:

> Was this learning? If so, was I learning because I was given the time to experience and discuss with others what I was thinking? Were my experiences becoming meaningful, useful, purposeful, continuous, incidental, collaborative (talk! talk! talk!), vicarious (great role models!), free of risk (it was OK to be a learner)? Did I need to be ready to learn how to learn again and feel what it feels like to be a learner? Did I need to feel the tension—the need to know and no longer be satisfied with what I did know?

For all of us, this process was reflexive. As we learned more about ourselves, we made connections back to our teaching. Susan, for example, having thought about herself as a learner and critically examined Frank Smith's theories, began to explore and make explicit her theory of learning. Having done so, she used her newly explicit (and revised) theory of learning to examine her classroom practices. Her theory also impacted the HT process she was using to better understand her students as learners; she noticed things she had not noticed before and she thought differently about what she saw. As Fran Yamate, a second-grade teacher, explained in her end-of-semester reflections paper:

> As I watched myself as a learner, I was reminded of things that had been taken for granted or long forgotten. . . . I noticed my excitement, curiosity, need to share ideas, and the sparks of interest that encouraged me to continue. I saw too the challenges and the exhilaration of making new discoveries. And, as I saw and understood myself as learner, I saw and understood myself more as teacher. The time I spent reading and thinking helped me rediscover and redefine my own values as a learner and as a teacher.

Time for Students to Be Learners

In traditional assessment, students are not engaged in self-assessment. In some forms of alternative assessment, students are explicitly asked to self-assess. The HT process is different. The process itself creates spaces for students to be learners. This happens because during everyday events, teachers begin to "step back" and watch and listen. Rather than fix, we try to understand. In doing so, we get out of the way of the students' learning. Initially, because we did not want to jump to "quick fixes," and because we were looking for multiple interpretations, we inadvertently gave students more time to solve their own problems. We subsequently came to value this time, time which Fran Yamate labels "discovery time—time for the child to figure out and use new strategies."

Because we valued this discovery time, we changed the shape of our responses. Rather than trying to solve problems for a particular child, we helped the child solve problems for himself or herself. This provides the child with more time to learn. As Dianne Yoshizawa, a kindergarten teacher, explained in a reflective paper she wrote,

> I found myself observing more and thinking about why a child does what he does, instead of directing him/her to do it my way. I also found myself asking a child to think through his/her actions so we could name and value them. I can see that by doing so, I give children the time and opportunity they need to think for themselves and make their own decisions.

HT also provides students with more time to be learners because teachers who use HT change their ways of teaching. Bette Ito, who teaches at a middle school, explains how she altered her role and her goals:

> I now want them to teach me what they know, how they have come to know that, and show me what they're going to do with that knowledge. . . .I now believe my job is to guide them beyond what they can already do. My students need to read for their own purposes and write in their own voice and answer their questions, not mine. They must discover how powerful their own voice can be. Because I've thought with the HT process, I've given back a lot of the responsibility for learning to them.

Making the "Abstraction Connection"

This term was coined by Lynn Yoshizaki, and many of us who have worked with Lynn have adopted the term because we have found it a useful way to placehold the third reason we value the HT process. Lynn explains that the "abstraction connection" happens when a learner gets "beneath the surface" and really understands. She says abstraction connections are "internalized understandings" and that making an abstraction connection is "like Thomas Edison's light bulb going on. Something clicks inside your brain. You get an 'aha!' and that feels so good."

We were able to make abstraction connections because we focused on understanding the "particular." As Elaine Tsuchiyama, a first-grade teacher, argues,

> It is the particulars that bring forth new understandings which help us make informed generalizations (abstraction connections). This idea of looking at the particulars of a child's learning is the driving force behind the HT process. It is the particulars that germinate possibilities that lead to new planes of understanding, making us, as learners, better teachers.
>
> With this newfound knowledge we then began to use what we had learned to help all the children in the classroom.

For all of us, the HT process allowed us to make abstraction connections. Things we knew, things that were somehow outside of us, became things we understood, things that were part of us. For many of us, this revolutionized how we thought and how we taught. Carrie Kawamoto, who was then teaching first grade, explains:

> As I listened to the children read, I could now see them making sense!! . . . Margaret Meek's [1987] words [about how books teach us to read] came alive for me. I had read her essay many times over the years but not until this year did her words make sense to me. I am now able to see the children learning to read with a new set of eyes.

A Fourth Reason?

There is, perhaps, a fourth reason, one that transcends all other reasons and, while simpler, is more complex: Using the HT process leaves us in a better place as teachers. All of us "ache with caring," all of us continually want to do a better job for children. We have seen that the HT process helps us do that. As Jennifer Story, a sixth-grade teacher, concluded:

> HT helps me begin the year feeling hopeful instead of helpless. I know that most of my kids, even the ones who have had bad school experiences, begin the year hoping that this year will be different, that this year they will be good and successful and that teachers will like them. It's obvious on the first day that all the children are trying to make a good first impression. It is only after they once again encounter the bitterness of failure that they begin to disrupt, call attention to

themselves, or resist through silence or non-cooperation. With HT, I hope to begin to find those students before they find me. Through my observations, I can be proactive instead of reactive, I can help my kids who need more help before they cry out for it, and, before they encounter failure again, perhaps I can introduce to them the sweet taste of success.

For all of us, this last reason is reason enough.

References Meek, M. (1988). *How texts teach what readers learn.* Stroud, England: Thimble Press.

Sciezka, J. (1989). *The true story of the three little pigs.* New York: Viking Children's Books.

Smith, F. (1988). *Understanding reading: A psycholinguistic analysis of reading and learning to read.* Hillsdale, NJ: Erlbaum.

Thaler, M. (1978). *There's a hippopotamus under my bed.* New York: Avon.

II Learning HT One-on-One

Introduction: How to Begin

Jennifer Story

Invites other teachers to try this process and explains this section's focus on novice teachers' experiences when first learning HT.

When teachers first begin to learn the HT process, they sometimes feel overwhelmed by the responsibility of knowing one child as a reader well enough to make a difference in the life of that child. They are more comfortable planning for and working with groups of children. Working one-on-one heightens their sense of responsibility and causes them to wonder if they indeed know enough to help this child, every child.

When I was first learning to think about one kid at a time, I found it helpful to follow the HT four-column list format. It helped me feel less overwhelmed. It gave structure to my thinking. It also provided a way to corral my need to be a panacea—to find a teacher solution for my kids, whose problems are actually very complex. As I grew used to HT as a way of thinking, I began to record data in my own ways, listing observations as narrative and hypotheses as questions. Over time, HT has evolved into an internalized thinking and record-keeping process, affecting how I think, write, and talk about my children and my actions in my classroom. I still keep formal notes and fall back on the structure when I need help in my thinking, in the same way I use a more formal lesson plan when I am trying something especially complex or experimental.

If you are new to the Hypothesis-Test process, the most important thing is to start at the beginning, with one child you are worried about. Don't think about that student at first, just record observations—the striking, the confusing, the questions you can't answer. Try not to figure out that kid in the beginning, just get to know the child, form a relationship, and absorb what you can learn from as many different angles as you can. The other important thing about HT is to

---

Parts of this introduction appeared in the January 1997 issue of *Primary Voices K–6*, under the title, "How to Begin" (p. 39).

think *with* someone else who wants to think with you. You can do HT by yourself, but alone you often dead-end, since you tend to answer your questions with the "solutions" you already knew.

So, what am I saying? Start out "as directed." Use the recipe. Follow the flow chart. Work with a buddy. Don't skip. Get the hang of it as a way of thinking by *doing* it. After you get the feel of it, you'll modify. But I think unless you really give it your best as it is laid out here, you might dismiss it as one of those "I tried that but it didn't work" techniques. HT is not an easy process to learn, but it is "teacher transforming."

Susan Oka-Yamashita, Lynn Yoshizaki, Elaine Tsuchiyama, and Diane Parker all feel that their lives as teachers were transformed both by what they learned from the HT process and how they learned it. In this section, they detail their experiences as "HT novices," explaining what it was like to learn the HT process working one-on-one with a child they worried about as a reader. They "walk" the reader through their semester-long experience; they detail their steps forward, back, and forward again. While most articles and book chapters are written from the perspective of the author who has finally "figured it all out," these chapters show the work it takes to figure something out, to learn something new. Our hope is that, by making public these experiences, the HT process becomes more accessible to readers than it would be if we detailed the subsequent, more "expert" experiences of these or other teachers.

Setera

Susan Oka-Yamashita
Mililani Waena Elementary School, Hawaii

Discusses how author learned HT while working with Setera, a second-grade child who began the year as a nonreader and ended the year as a beginning reader. Helps the reader see what progress looks like when a child's reading behaviors are more consistent with those of a child who is chronologically younger.

Setera wrote in his Communication Log, "Itat I VPBKE." Looking past me, away from his writing, he read what he wrote: "I learned about animals and I like the skeleton." I wasn't worried because it was just the beginning of the school year, and I had a few other students who were writing random letters. Other children had started their second-grade year that way.

Setera read a book to me. He selected *Rooster's Off to See the World* by Eric Carle (1972). He said the book was about a rooster and his friend, but could not tell me the title or author. He said he chose the book because of the "nice colors." As he read, I noticed that his words did not match the words in the book; his eyes were focused on the top corner of the page, away from the text (Setera's words appear in regular print; the text as written in the book appears immediately beneath it in bold italics):

> One rooster, he was alone. He did not have no friends.
> ***One fine morning, a rooster decided that he wanted to travel. So, right then and there, he set out to see the world. He hadn't walked very far when he began to feel lonely.***
>
> It is everybody here tonight? A frog and the turtle and the fishes wanted to go home except the rooster.
> ***The sun went down. It began to get dark.***
>
> (The subsequent pages of the text show each animal complaining about food or shelter.)
>
> The rooster was sad and he went to sleep. The end.
> ***After a while he went to sleep and had a wonderful happy dream—all about a trip around the world!***

I asked Setera, "How did you know that the rooster was sad?" Setera replied, "His face looked sad." "How did you know the rooster went to sleep?" I continued. He responded, "Because I saw it in the picture. He looks like a ball when he sleeps."

I was puzzled but thought to myself, "Don't panic. It's OK, he's not reading the words on the page but telling his own story from the picture. It sounds as if he's familiar with or has heard the story before. It's sort of OK, I guess, but . . . At least he seems to be enjoying his reading."

But then again, he was in the second grade and should be able to read and write more conventionally, right? Instead, in many ways, he was reading and writing like my own two children, Ren, age 4½, and Joy, 2. They could tell a story from pictures; they could write random letters. What was going on?

I decided I needed to find out more about Setera's history as a student. Cumulative folder? Nothing. Report card? Comments cut off, grades average. Title 1 teacher at his previous school did not remember him. Mother? "He's my baby, the only child at home. His two sisters are older and not living at home. Last year, he cried a lot. He cried when he couldn't do the work. During first grade at his other school, they worked on lots of math sheets at home." "What about his reading?" I asked. "I only saw math homework."

Standardized tests? We'd given him the MAT (Metropolitan Achievement Test) to determine if he should receive Title 1 services. Based on his scores, he qualified. The part that puzzled me was that he did really well on the first page. He attended to the print and answered appropriately. However, he didn't do well on subsequent pages. I wondered if he had made some lucky guesses on the first page.

Behavior in class? I noticed that he sat on the outskirts of the class, and was not disruptive to those around him. In a group, he would be there physically but usually on the side, watching, not attempting to interact or be part of the group. He had no friends that he interacted with regularly.

I didn't find any one thing that struck me as being *particularly* unusual, but I still felt there was something more to understand about Setera. Could he write last year? Could he read last year? Did something happen over the summer that caused change? Was he overlooked last year because he didn't create a disturbance, or call attention to himself? Did his crying when he felt he couldn't do a task create a situation where he was left alone? I had no answers.

Reading, and helping children to enjoy reading, is important to me. Although Setera appeared to enjoy looking through books and telling stories from pictures, Setera was not looking at or trying to read printed text. That puzzled me.

I decided to keep reading particularly enjoyable and nonthreatening for Setera so that he would pay attention to print and enjoy reading. As a class, we read many poems and songs from the children's song books, and from chart paper. During shared reading time, I decided to pair Setera with more fluent readers, or someone he selected to read with. I wanted him to be reading along with others so he could hear other people. I had him read books of his own choice by himself and with others. I asked him and those reading with him to point to words as they read. I even asked some of my better readers to share with him what they did as they read a book. But he continued to "read" only the pictures. I was very frustrated!

In writing, I worked with him, asking him to dictate words to me, and then copy it to his paper. I had him dictate his words to his classmates, and then copy it to his paper. I also had him work along-side others as they wrote. But even this type of writing was difficult for him. I wrote his words on a paper: "I read the book *Santa's Cookie Surprise*. It was a fun book."

He copied: "I read the book *Santa Surprise*. It was a fun"

I asked him, "What happened to the rest of the words?" He replied, "It didn't fit." I asked him to write it again, but this time to continue the words that didn't fit on the next line. He came back with the same results.

I told myself to be patient and to give him time. Everybody learns at their own pace, but still, I was worried.

What else was there for me to try? How and what might I do to get him to engage with text so he could make meaning from print? What did I know? I was now in my third year of teaching, feeling very wet behind the ears. I was still struggling to understand how students learn, period!

Around this time, I started taking a year-long reading course on how children learn to use language. However, the course (taught by Dr. Diane Stephens at our school on Saturdays) couldn't give me what I needed. I wanted immediate answers so that I could begin to help Setera before too much time passed. I didn't have all year! I shared my concerns with Diane and my group, but no one could offer any quick fixes (or even longer ones).

I really wanted something or someone to tell me exactly what to do to "fix" what puzzled me, but I knew from my previous experiences that I would not find it. After all, I had all the teacher manuals for language, reading, and writing, and none could say its way was *the* way.

Since we were learning to use miscue analysis in Diane's class, I taped Setera reading. Although the stories he read were too short to do miscue [*Rain* (Kalan, 1978), *Have You Seen My Cat?* (Carle, 1973) and *I Wish I Could Fly* (Maris, 1986)], his "reading" told me that he had heard the stories before. His eyes focused on the picture on the page, not the text. He was familiar enough with the story line to use the pictures to tell a story. When I asked him how he knew what was said, he would say "from the picture," or point to the picture. When I pointed to a word, he quickly glanced away. It was as if he was afraid of the words! What was I to do? Was there something wrong with his eyes?

At Diane's recommendation, I used Marie Clay's *Sand—The Concepts about Print Test* (1972) to understand what Setera knew as a reader. While going through the prescribed activities, he said that parts of the text and pictures were "down side up" or "up side up," but even when prompted with "What's wrong on this page?" he did not say that the pictures or text were upside down, or the words were spelled incorrectly or in a funny order. When asked to point to a word, he pointed to a letter; when asked to point to two words, he pointed to two letters in one word. Were words and letters the same to him?

Then I asked Setera to read the story for me. His eyes focused on the picture on the right-hand page and seemed to avoid the text on the left-hand page. He read slowly and carefully, as if trying to pull the words from his head, creating text as he went along to describe the action in the picture. The following is taken from a transcript of his reading:

> I dug a little hole in the sand.
> *I took a little spade and I dug a little hole.*
>
> The water was in the hole.
> *I dug a little hole and the waves splashed in.*
>
> (Subsequent pages explain that the boy dug a bigger hole, waves splashed in, and he jumped in the hole. He wondered what could float in the hole and what he could make with the sand. His mother called him and told him it was time to come home and he did.)
>
> Next week he looked for da hole. All he saw was dry sand, corn sand, and wet sand, and black sand.
> *On another day I looked for that hole. All I saw was flat sand, soft sand, wet sand, and waves. But oh, no hole!*
>
> [Silence] "Oh!?" [Silence]
> *The waves splashed in the hole.*

Setera's voice echoed with surprise. There were no pictures on the page. He did not "read" it. I think I was as surprised as he was at his reaction.

Setera seemed to make connections from the pictures to what he knew, but seemed stymied when there were no pictures. Why did that happen? Why did he rely so heavily on pictures? Why did Setera seem to avoid looking at print, both in books and his own? It just did not make sense to me.

What should I do? Should I refer him for screening and special services? I continued to talk about him with Diane and my group. He puzzled them also. He was not responding to whatever suggestions had been made. I decided to continue reading and writing with him within the context of the classroom, and keep our exchanges friendly and nonthreatening. I encouraged him to read predictable books. However, nothing I did seemed to really help. I wanted him to actively engage with, understand and make meaning from print, understand sound–symbol relationships, to read and write like a second grader. Maybe he didn't want this? He seemed neither curious nor enthusiastic about books. I kept comparing him to my own two preschool-aged children who were teaching themselves about reading, about sound–symbol relationships. They seemed to want to figure it out. Didn't Setera feel the same way?

An Inquiry Is Born

During one of our Saturday sessions, Diane introduced HT as a way of thinking through our observations. I was puzzled by what she was saying. She asked us to make an observation of a student, and to find five or more interpretations (possible reasons) for that observation. That seemed next to impossible!

I looked back at the interpretations I'd made based on Setera's reading of *Sand* (Clay, 1972). I saw that what I'd done was quickly come up with surface-level interpretations. For example, I had initially thought:

> Setera is unable to decode.
>
> Print has no meaning.
>
> He is unaware of print on page.
>
> He will get extra attention if he can't read.
>
> He thinks it is more fun to read the pictures and make up his own story.

Diane, however, worked with me to stretch my thinking. I had to dig beneath the surface and find deeper causes for what I observed. I had to look at the situation with different, more expanded perspectives. It was no longer, "OK, Student A is doing this. This is why, and this is what we will do." This new process helped me see a wider range of possibilities. I eventually came up with these interpretations:

> Was it easier for him to talk than to read text?
>
> Was he interested only in the visual, but not print, information?
>
> Was it that he did not understand sound–symbol correspondence?
>
> Was it that he did not understand that print is meaningful?
>
> Was it that he did not understand the role of print in meaning making?
>
> Did he think that "reading" was telling a story from the pictures?
>
> Was reading my agenda, not his?

Around that time, I received an invitation to work with Diane in the project we named Engagements. As a part of Engagements, I would work one-on-one with a child from my classroom. There was no doubt in my mind who I would work with. I needed help understanding how to work with Setera. I knew it wouldn't be easy, but I wanted to make sense of what I was seeing. (Example 2, on pages 31–33, shows some of the different ways I tried to make sense of my work with Setera.)

Diane explained that during the one-on-one time, my job was to invite Setera into the learning, pay attention to how he learns, and find the best ways to meet his needs, while keeping the focus on literacy. I needed to make sure that each Engagements session included writing and reading, although it didn't need to be labeled that. I needed to follow his lead. How in the world would I do that? What would I do for one hour? What would engage him? What would make him feel OK about using printed text to read and write? What would help him understand that print is meaningful?

I decided to invite Setera to bring books and whatever he wanted to share with me to the first session. I also decided to bring books, games, and whatever I felt might interest him. At that first session, Setera said, "I forgot to bring my book." I asked him to look through the class books and he selected one about animals. We sat with our backs to everyone else since he chose to sit in the corner. We spent most of the time talking. I tried to get to know him and to find out about his interests. He used simple sentences to tell about himself, and his responses to my questions were focused. We shared the book together and talked about it, and we built with pattern blocks. Then he wrote a short note about what we did that morning:

> IB-eDmm
> IbeAeBmmFS
>   Setera.

Without looking at what he had written, he read, "Dear Mom, I worked with blocks and I builded all kinds of things and I had great ideas. I builded gates. I'm building different color gates. Setera."

The HT Cycle Begins

For the second session, I decided to try to understand Setera's thinking. I asked him what he thought a reader was and how he thought people learned to read and write. Setera said he didn't know: "I can't read. I don't know how. I never learned. Nobody teaching me. I can't write. I don't know how." When I asked him how he decided what letters to write, he said he chose "easy" ones.

Based on these observations, I generated several possible interpretations:

Did Setera think reading is something that needs to be taught?

Did he think that someone "forgot" to teach him how to read?

Does Setera see that others read/write "faster" and so he tries to copy them?

Does he understand that letters are ways to place-hold meaning?

Does he lack confidence in himself as a reader/writer?

Rather than try to construct a hypothesis at this point, I decided to gather more information. I talked to his mom, who said that she and Setera read a lot at home. I asked Setera to show me how he read to his mom. He said he read "by sounding it out." I again asked him to show me. He sat there, looked at the book, then tried to sound out the letters individually. It was difficult to hear him, and he wasn't able to put the letters together to make one word. Maybe that was why he couldn't read. Now I had a hypothesis: Maybe Setera's only successful strategy was looking at pictures. To test this out, I decided to observe Setera more when he read. Based on those observations, I soon became pretty sure that this was true. Setera even explained his strategy to another student: He was reading *All I Am* (Roe, 1990) with Kevin. I heard Kevin say, "I am a ga-ga . . . ga-ra . . ." Setera said, "Just look at the picture if you don't know what that word is. It looks like a dad so that word is 'dad'" [it was grandfather].

In our sessions and in the classroom, Setera continued to represent his ideas with a string of random letters. He did not use spaces between the letters to represent words. I tried to find a way to get him to pay attention to print. Sometimes we had simple written conversations. I would write him and draw a picture. He would write back and draw a picture, I would respond. We would read the conversations together, pointing to the words. We also made lists. I kept track of observations, and made interpretations and hypotheses. I was soon pretty sure that his understanding of sound–symbol relationships was limited. He often would write only the most dominant sound he could identify.

One day, for example, he wrote to me (see Figure 2): IetPetoealtVetp to mokooka mro mrsoka. When I asked him to read it to me, his eyes looked away from the paper as he read, "I had fun playing with the game with you that I saw on TV. It was fun, that game was fun. To Mrs. Oka."

"Who is this from?"

"Oops," he responded, and turned the paper over and wrote *Setera.*

I then asked him to circle each word for me. He circled as he read, ran out of letters to match his words, and promptly added more letters. I asked, "Read it again for me?" He read, "I had fun playing

Figure 2.
Setera's note and drawing for
author, with her transcription of
Setera's reading of the text.

with the game with you. It was fun. To Mrs. Oka. This is from Setera."
Based on my observations and interpretations of this and other events
that occurred that day, I hypothesized that he was beginning to
understand the relationship between what was written and what was
read/said.

Example 2. The author experimented with the format of her HT sheets. Sometimes Susan worked with a narrative form (see Example 2a). Other times, she kept all similar observations clustered together in a computer file and would revisit those observations (see Example 2b), which she then would use to generate interpretations (2c) and hypotheses (2d) and to confirm "pretty sures" (2e).

2a

Then I did my note and picture for him. I asked him if he shared the note with his mother. He said yes. What did she say? He didn't reply. Today he wrote me, *IetPetoealtVetp to mokooka mro mrsok*, which he read as "I had fun playing with the game with you that I saw on TV. It was fun, that game was fun. To Mrs. Oka."

He had originally written *to mok* and said, "I forgot how to spell your name." While I finished up my note and picture to him, he added the rest of the letters, copying from what I was writing. He tried to copy my picture and draw me sitting down. Then he said he made a mistake and drew it on the back. This time I am standing up. My right arm has two sections, my left arm has three sections. He passed it to me and then said "Oops" and took it back. He said, "I forgot your feet." I asked him how I would know who this was from and he wrote on the back side of the sheet *Setera*. I asked him to read me what he wrote again and he said, "I had fun playing the game with you. It was fun. This is from Setera."

Interpretations
1. Does Setera understand sound–symbol relationships?
2. Does Setera have confidence in himself as a writer?
3. Does it matter to him that he is able to communicate in writing?
4. Is writing "painful" for him?
5. Does he have strategies for making sense of print?
6. Does he understand that written language is different from speech?

2b

Observations

1. October: Setera "read" *Rooster's Off to See the World* to me. Since he doesn't yet read the printed text of a story, he told his own story based on the visual pictoral clues. He was reading with another student and when that person needed to decode for me, Setera would tell them just to look at the pictures if they didn't know what the word said.

2. December: In Marie Clay's *Concepts of Print* test, Setera focused on the picture to "read" the story. On last page where there was no picture, he made a sound of surprise or dismay (?). He didn't seem to know what to do and said that there was not a picture. When asking about words and letters, he showed one and two letters as representing both words and letters.

3. 1/14: Setera looked through the book *Many Luscious Lollipops* page by page. At each page, he would name what he saw, count how many and compare, match similar objects, etc. I would try to read to him what was on the page by pointing to the words. As I did this, he would turn the page and start to talk about what he saw on the next page. He looked at pictures and talked about what was on the different pages but unless asked to, he avoided focusing on the print on the page.

4. 1/19: He participated in "cooperative reading" when the class read a rhyme called "Families." The class had read it together a few times. He was Child 2. Mrs. Oshiro helped him get started by saying "Quack, quack, quack, quack." He mumble-read with her, "Quack, quack, quack, quack . . . Madame, I've got eight. Three of them are yellow . . ." On his own he recited, "Three of them are brown, two of them are snowy white" and ended using mumble-reading "the prettiest in the town."

5. 1/26: Mumble-reading is used while reading our class song book. He participates by reading what is written by mumbling along with the class. While reading his part in the play *January Is the First Month*, he also did this.

5a. 1/26: Setera brought a *Levitt's (?) Encyclopedia* to share with me. The shark page was placemarked with some worksheets. We talked about the different sharks and what he knew about them. As he told me what he knew, I would skim the text to see if the remark was appropriate. I would also say things like, "Gee, here it talks about such-and-such shark. Let's see what it says," or "Let me read what it says here about the shark." I would read the text and try to get him to focus on the print. He looked in the direction of the page, but his eyes did not necessarily look at what I was pointing at.

5b. 1/26: The first book he picked up was a comparison of sharks and fishes, sharks and man, etc. I tried reading parts of the book and pointing to the words as I read, especially after he would say something about the picture. While there didn't seem to be an avoidance of print, there did seem to be disinterest in their purpose and meaning. For example, he asked why there was a man swimming. I read the line which said to look at the size, but he didn't seem to understand what the words meant and continued to wonder out loud why. I found information about the sharks we had been talking about and read it to him. I also tried to get him to read some of the names of the sharks but he would tell me he didn't know.

5c. 1/26: Setera said he was going to draw a basking shark in blue. I asked him to write the name of the shark he drew. He copied from the book, "Great White Shark."

5d. 1/26: He told me they saw lizards in the book and he tried to locate it but wasn't able to find it. He saw pictures of shipbuilding and said that the pictures were boats. He was not able to tell me that the encyclopedia had information on things beginning with *S*.

(continued)

5e. 1/26: I asked him how he knew this book was on sharks. His reply was because of the pictures. He also pulled out books on fishes, saying they were about sharks. He did find picutres within the book of sharks.

6. *Puzzle:* In September/October (?) when they were given the MET, Gay said that he did really well on the first page, he attended to the print and answered appropriately. However, subsequent pages did not turn out as well.

7. 2/1: Setera sat at his desk with his song book closed. He did not open or look at it until directed to do so. He did not attempt to follow along with his eyes or by pointing to the words with his fingers. He just sat there and looked around. He closed his book after one rhyme was read and didn't open it again even if we were reading another rhyme. He didn't fully participate when they sang *Jingle Bell Rock*. His mouth moved some of the time as he looked around the room.

8a. 2/2: I attempted throughout the session to get him to focus on the printed text by asking questions such as, "What is this game called? Can you point to the name of the game? What are the men called? Where can we find out what pieces are in this box? How can we find out how to play the game? How many players can play the game at one time?" etc, but most questions fell on deaf ears.

8b. 2/2: I tried to see if we could get the name of the game by what he knew about "towers." He did mention the word *tower* but in another context. I tried to draw it out again but wasn't able to. I told him you said the word *tower,* is this a tower? He nodded. Then I asked him what was the tower doing. He said things like "falling, shaking." I pointed to the *T* in *Tipsy* and asked him what that would sound like. Did it sound like any of the words he said? I finally pointed to the name *Tipsy Tower* and said it out loud. He repeated it and looked at it while I pointed to "Tipsy Tower" on the box and on the game [it's all around the rims of each level]. He repeated it and pointed to it himself along the levels. He asked while pointing, "Does this say *Tipsy Tower? . . . Tipsy Tower?*"

8c. 2/2: About halfway through the period and in the midst of playing with the game, Setera took out a book called *Shark Mania*. He turned to the page that talked about the nose of the shark, saying that the shark has sharp teeth. How did he know? He pointed to the picture of the shark. He also said that the shark was a great white (I don't think it was). The page was about "Noses? . . . Some sharks have sharp teeth. . ." We looked through the book and talked about different pages. Each time he would tell me something or ask me something about the shark, I would skim the text to verify and ask him how he knew. His accounts were not what the text said usually. I read along with him, pointing to the text as I read, and asking him if he recognized any words. I read some of the words (such as shark, nose, teeth) and asked him if he could find the word *shark* on the page. He was able to only after prompting. He could not read *noses* but knew that n-o was *no.* I asked him what on his face started with that sound. After a while he was able to say "nose."

2c

Interpretations

From Observation

1,2,3,4,5e	Is Setera relying heavily or interested in visual but not print information?
1,2,3,5e	Does Setera understand that print is meaningful?
1,5,5d-e	Does not have strategies for making sense of print.
1,2,3,5e,7	Does not willingly engage with print.
1	Does Setera understand that written language is different from speech?
1,4,8c	Is the material familiar from prior experience?
2,3,4,6	Does he really read and comprehend but doesn't want to show us he can?
2,6	Does he really read and comprehend but doesn't see the value of it, so doesn't?
2,3	Does Setera understand sound-to-speech correspondence?
3,5d-e	Does he make connections to what he knows and pictures in text?
3,5d	Does Setera feel it is easier to talk than to read and write?
3,7	Is there too much distraction in the classroom for Setera to focus?
3	Words don't have meaning—look like a jumble of letters or symbols.
4	Has he "memorized" text from previous readings?
4,7	Does he have strategies for reading independently?
4	Does Setera have confidence in himself as a reader?
5	Is risk taking hard to do?
5b,7	Does it matter to Setera if he is able to read?
5b	Does Setera expect to fail each time he reads?
5b,7	Has Setera had negative reading experiences in earlier years?
5b-e	Does Setera have an understanding of what words mean?
5b	Does he have a concept of size relationships—spatial?
5b	Are pictures too abstract?
5c	Does Setera effectively use environmental print to help him write?
5c	Does not have a variety of strategies as a writer.
5c	Does he have strategies as a writer but doesn't use them flexibly?
5d-e	Is he telling me what he thinks based on the pictures he's seen?

(continued)

2c, continued

5d,8b-c	Does not understand sound–symbol relationships.
5,5a,8b-c	Is Setera going along with the "game" and doing what he thinks I want him to do?
6	Was the test too long so he lost his focus/attention?
6	Has he figured out that he gets more attention this way, so sticks to this behavior?
6	Did he just make some lucky guesses on the first page?
6,7,8a	Is there too much visual information presented at one time in printed text so that Setera is overwhelmed and unable to sort through and focus?
6,7,8a	Does Setera have enough nonvisual information to discriminate between a letter and a word?
6,7,8a	Does Setera read environmental print?
8a	Was he ignoring me because he was concentrating on "exploring" first?
8a	Is he aware that there was print on the box (the box is colorful, text was white letters on blue background)?
8a	Is he able to see the print on the box? Is it too small?
8a	Was the box too "busy" so he could not focus?
8a	Did he need to know the name of the game or the game rules?
8a	Was I pushing too hard to get him to attend?
8b-c	Does he understand the words *Tipsy Tower*?
8b-c	Does he see that he can (potentially) use print info, "unlock the code"?
8b-c	Does he see that print can be helpful to him?
8c	Is he developing a small sight vocabulary?
8c	Was he "bored" with the game because of my questioning so he thought he would change the "subject"?
8c	Is he interested in sharks so he could identify the written word?
8c	Was I questioning too much, so he thought he would change the subject?

2d

Hypotheses

From Observation

4	Does Setera exhibit reading-like behavior?
5	Will Setera take more risks/be more successful with language if we work with his interests?
5	Is print meaningful and does it make sense?
3	Setera may not understand the role of print in meaning making.
3	Under what conditions and in what situations will Setera "read"?
3	Has Setera learned that others will "do" for him—dependency?
3	Does Setera have strategies as a reader/writer?
3	Does Setera feel more comfortable with "talk" than with print? How much stronger are verbal skills?
3	Under what conditions will Setera focus?

2e

Pretty Sure

Setera doesn't yet "read" the story (or printed text). He tells his own version based on pictorial clues. He can participate in reading using a combination of the strategies (such as mumble-reading and cooperative reading) described by David Doake in *Reading-Like Behavior: Its Role in Learning to Read.*

Setera does not understand the role of print in meaning making (in text and his own).

Around this same time, I began to have enough data (observations) to confirm an earlier hypothesis. I became pretty sure that whenever Setera was engaged in a literacy (reading and writing) experience, he would exhibit what I called avoidance behavior: He would stretch his arms, yawn, sometimes loudly, scratch his body, and rub his eyes. It didn't matter if it were a book he brought and wanted to read. If we were reading together, or he was reading with a classmate, he would, at times, engage in Doake's (1988) "mumble-reading" and "cooperative reading," but his eyes scanned the horizon as he mouthed the words. Sometimes he would just begin talking about something that popped into his mind to whoever was next to him. I wanted to understand this pattern. My curricular decision was to continue to observe him. Under what conditions would he engage with text?

In February, I watched as Setera sat between two classmates reading Robert Munsch's *Love You Forever* (1986), a book he said he liked to read. But Setera sat, eyes scanning the room, hands in his lap or on the side, as his classmates read. When it was his turn to read, he held the book in front of his face. His eyes focused on the pictures as he "read" the words to the story—his own words. I started to read with him and pointed to the words as I read them. Setera echoed me as I read repetitious parts. I continued to read when he hesitated. Parts he knew, he recited along with the others, "I'll love you forever, I'll like you for always, As long as I'm living, My baby you'll be." But he never looked at the words. His eyes scanned the room. I generated these interpretations:

> Was this familiar text, so that Setera was able to read with some prompting?
>
> Did Setera not want to risk showing that he could not read?
>
> Was print, even in familiar text, not meaningful to Setera?
>
> Was there too much text on the page?
>
> Did he not understand the relationship between what was said ("reading") and what was on the page?

Diane suggested that I read *Understanding Reading* by Frank Smith (1988). I had a hard time reading his book, but was more challenged to stay with it because he said it was OK to put it down if it was too hard. I struggled to understand what he meant when he said:

> Reading is possible only when the reader can bring sufficient nonvisual information [prior knowledge] to bear to reduce the amount of visual information that must be attended to in the text, or at least to utilize the visual information [new knowledge] as economically and efficiently as possible. (p. 178)

Was Setera experiencing what Smith calls "visual overload," with "too much new or foreign information to look at [so] it becomes overwhelming and we withdraw"? Was it possible that Setera did not have enough prior experiences with text to help him feel comfortable with a new or different situation? Was it possible that some books had too much text on a page so Setera shut down?

Wow! I had never thought of it that way. Looking back on my observations, I realized that Setera's avoidance behaviors occurred whenever he read books that had more than a few words on a page. I decided to try using books from the Wright Group (The Story Box) because of their short story line. Would he be more successful reading these? Would he actively engage with these and "read"?

Setera seemed happy and excited when introduced to these books. He chose to read *What's for Lunch?* (Williams, 1990b), *Where Are They Going?* (Williams, 1990c), and *On a Chair* (Williams, 1990a). We talked about what the books might be about and how he knew. I shared my connections to the pictures and story. As he read, Setera did not attend to print unless told to. He looked in the direction of the text but would not look directly at the words. While pointing to words and reading, he skimmed his fingers over the words and did not make that one-to-one correspondence. These observations, combined with all the observations I had made already, confirmed for me my hypothesis that Setera did not yet consistently understand the relationship between what was "read" and the print on the page. These observations also led to new questions/interpretations:

Was he resorting to avoidance behavior because he was not sure he could be successful?

Was he resorting to avoidance behavior because he was working with something new?

Was there still too much text on a page, even with only one line?

Was it still too early for him to take a risk as a reader?

Were we working on areas of interest to Setera?

Still Searching

I continued to use these books because I was pretty sure that longer books would cause an even stronger avoidance reaction. I had him choose the books he wanted to read, and I read with him, asking him to point to the words as he said them to help him make the print-to-sound connection. I encouraged him to continue to use picture clues to help him decode text, because I noticed that he read much better when he didn't try to sound out the words. These curricular decisions were all based on my being pretty sure that he did not yet consistently understand the relationship between what was said and what was read, and that his knowledge of sound–symbol relationships was too weak for him to rely effectively on sounding out.

Near the end of the study, Setera was reading a very short predictable book, *My Senses* (Ditzel, 1992). By this time, I was quite sure that Setera was using multiple strategies to make meaning from print. He consistently demonstrated his understanding of the relationship between what was written and what was read. For example, in one story, he didn't quite understand the word *senses* but he knew it had something to do with people because of the picture on the cover.

> *Setera:* (reading slowly) I use my . . . [looked at the picture] ears. I know it's ears because [pointing to the picture of the ocean] to hear? [looking at me for confirmation] the [his eyes again scanned the picture] to hear the sea? . . . It's sea because the boy is listening to the shell.
>
> *Susan:* I use my ears to hear the waves.
>
> *Setera:* (turning the page, with a smile, slowly reading) I use my [quick look at the picture] mouth to. . . What's that word [pointing to smell]?
>
> *Susan:* Smell.
>
> *Setera:* Oh . . . I use my nose to smell. (Commenting on his reading) The lines looked like they were coming from his mouth, but the lines were going up to his nose.

I was very pleased. In this short passage, he'd made a connection, reread, and corrected for meaning!

Another time, he wrote "Aja S..... fite." [Aja and Sasha fight.] I could see him sounding out the individual words as he wrote. He explained: "I can write Aja's but not Sasha's name." I told him that using the *S* to remind him it was about Sasha was a good idea. I also told him he did a good job on the word *fight*. "Did I spell it right?" he wanted to know. "Almost, it does sound like that, and that's great," I replied. I showed him the conventional spelling. Setera broke into a big smile.

I wondered what would happen once our one-to-one Engagements sessions ended in April. He had been making considerable progress—would he do as well in a classroom setting? I continued to work with Setera daily, reading and writing, trying to sustain what had been achieved. He continued to try to read from printed text, and he began to seek classmates' help when he needed words spelled. He volunteered to read books to the class, and he would be the reporter on the daily news.

Then summer came and Setera left for another school, and, a year later so did I.

When I think about Setera then and now, I think about myself and my role. When he was in second grade with me, he and I made considerable progress. And then the year ended. Could I have done more? I ask myself a lot of questions about my teaching. I make myself the subject of the HT process—reflecting on what I did or didn't do, sifting through interpretations of why, and what I could do—trying to imagine, as Ralph Peterson (1992) says, "what is, what should or ought to be, and what could be, or is possible."

I learned a lot about literacy from working with Setera. I learned a lot about myself. I learned to look at what I did in the classroom to facilitate learning and what kinds of messages I sent the children. I learned to watch my students closely as learners and to reflect carefully on what I observed. I also learned that I can't fix or solve everything. I can't make everything "right." This was the hardest lesson of all. Diane warned us against "quick fixes," but still I wanted to fix Setera. But HT isn't about fixing children: it is about understanding them enough to try to help.

References

Carle, E. (1972). *Rooster's off to see the world.* New York: Scholastic.

Carle, E. (1973). *Have you seen my cat?* New York: F. Watts.

Clay, M. (1972). *Sand—the concepts about print test.* Auckland, New Zealand: Heinemann Educational Books.

Craig, J. (1989). *Santa's cookie surprise,* Mahwah, NJ: Troll Associates.

Ditzel, R. (1992). *My senses.* Honolulu, HI: Bess Press.

Doake, D. (1988). *Reading begins at birth.* Richmond Hill, Ontario: Scholastic.

Kalan, R. (1978). *Rain.* New York: Greenwillow Books.

Maris, R. (1986). *I wish I could fly.* New York: Greenwillow Books.

Munsch, R. (1986). *Love you forever.* Scarborough, Ontario: Firefly Books.

Peterson, R. (1992). *Life in a crowded place: Making a learning community.* Portsmouth, NH: Heinemann.

Roe, E. (1990). *All I am.* New York: Bradbury Press.

Smith, F. (1988). *Understanding reading: A psycholinguistic analysis of reading and learning to read.* Hillsdale, NJ: Erlbaum.

Williams, R. (1990a). *On a chair.* Bothell, WA: The Wright Group.

Williams, R. (1990b). *What's for lunch?* Bothell, WA: The Wright Group.

Williams, R. (1990c). *Where are they going?* Bothell, WA: The Wright Group.

Joshua

Lynn Yoshizaki
Wahiawa Elementary School, Hawaii

Describes how author used HT to help Joshua transform himself in both fifth and sixth grades.

"Why do we have school?"
"How will I know when real learning has taken place?"
"Am I an effective teacher?"

Searching. Searching. Searching. Since I began teaching in 1969, I have been trying to understand teaching and learning. I've felt a gnawing discomfort and sought long and hard to understand that discomfort. I'd ask myself, "Is real learning taking place? How do I know if it is?" To help me gain that beneath-the-surface understanding of teaching and its connection to real learning, I tried different professional assignments: classroom teacher, floating teacher, early childhood program coordinator, teacher of students identified as gifted and talented in math, workshop instructor. I went to countless staff development sessions on reading, art, math, science, social studies, total quality learning, philosophy for children, whole language, teachers as researchers, and alternative assessment. I joined teacher study groups. Nothing seemed to soothe my discomfort.

Then I was asked to participate in a project called Engagements, sponsored by the school's Title 1 program. The facilitator would be Dr. Diane Stephens, from the University of Hawaii. I was excited: I was going to work directly with a professor! I love challenges—and perhaps I could find out what had been bothering me for all these years.

Before jumping in, I asked many questions about the requirements, the instructor, and the logistics. I got typical answers: "Oh, you just have to work with a student." "The prof is really nice." "You'll be working with your colleagues." "We'll hire subs for you." "You won't need to worry about your class." This left me a little nervous but my appetite was whetted; I wanted to be part of the project. Little did I know the magnitude of work ahead of me—nor the frustrations, the exasperation, the burning candles at both ends into the night—or the inspirations, discoveries, and enduring friendships I found!

We began in January 1994. I was asked to choose a student I was worried about, and I immediately thought of Joshua, one of my fifth-grade students. I was puzzled by him. A slight, pleasant looking fellow,

Joshua was an American of African and Japanese ancestry. School was hard for him. Academically, he functioned like a beginning second grader. In addition, classmates would complain constantly about him. "Mrs. Y., Joshua's teasing me." "Mrs. Y., Joshua took my pencil." "Mrs. Y., Joshua's writing on my paper." "Mrs. Y., Joshua's going to beat me up at recess." *Joshua, barely four feet tall and 54 pounds, going to beat up a five feet three, 120 pound boy?* Joshua, on the other hand, would whine about others teasing him or blame someone for distracting him from his work. It was annoying and disruptive!

In spite of his behavior, I liked Joshua. I felt a kinship with him. He was able to hold his own in conversations with me. I found his sense of humor inviting. He picked up on my plays on language. Sometimes you could see him sharing the jokes with his classmates and they'd all have a good laugh together. I felt he was more capable than he appeared. It didn't seem as if he should be failing.

Our first session was in early January. We began by talking about working and learning together: "I would like to help you learn to read better. I'm learning about how to help kids learn to read. So I'll be learning with you." Joshua thought that was OK. "What would you like to talk about?" I asked.

"My mother is sick," he began. "She may die. She has a brain tumor. She's been sick with a terminal brain condition for a long time. I remember going to the hospital a lot because my mom would black out, fall, and hurt herself. She has a wheelchair now to help her move around. I worry a lot about my mom because I know she will die soon. My brother and I, we don't have a father living with us. My mom and dad got a divorce because he would beat her when he got drunk and mad. I remember running away to the shelter because we were afraid my dad would kill my mom. When I get angry, I throw things."

I was shocked into silence. What a tremendous burden for him to bear. Here was a young man, age 10, going through such heart-wrenching experiences. How did he deal with such fear, anger, and sadness? No wonder he had difficulty in school. It seemed miraculous that he came to school as much as he did. I needed to help him, I wanted to help him—but where to begin? How would I help him?

Joshua took three full one-hour sessions to finish talking about himself and his family. Eventually he began talking about his heritage. He spoke of his interest in learning about Japan. We looked at some books on Japan and did some origami, the Japanese art of paper folding. We worked hard on following the illustrated directions in the book. When we made a mistake, we joked about it and simply tried again. The origami sessions lasted for three weeks.

During this time, I was starting to learn about the HT process. First, I needed to learn to write down what I observed, not what I *thought* about what I observed. Then, I needed to come up with at least five interpretations for each observation. Initially, I struggled with this. Recording observations taught me to see, but learning to observe was hard. I wrote to Diane:

> I am having difficulty differentiating the "worthy" observations/ interpretations. Should I be setting up some kind of criteria in my mind to help myself? Or would this detract from truly observing/ interpreting? When you talk about the undergrads (and their struggles with this), I feel like one of them because I don't feel confident about what to write. Sometimes I think I am grasping it and then it eludes me.

By the eighth session with Joshua, I felt as if I was beginning to have a handle on observations and interpretations. Diane's responses to my journal and to my HT sheet were helping me expand my interpretations. However, I still wasn't sure what a hypothesis should look like or what a curricular decision was.

Meanwhile, Joshua and I continued to learn more about origami and about Japan. I felt that Joshua was beginning to trust me; he began to ask for help when he needed it. We began bonding as co-

---

What Is It Like to Use the HT Process?

Using HT is like trying on a new hat, except that you are trying on a new way of thinking.

You know how to put on a hat. You know it goes on your head. You struggle to make it fit comfortably and look just right. You try various ways to fit it on your head. At first, you quickly pull it down and make it fit the contours of your head like a quick fix. Then you let it sit loosely and allow it to ride on your head, haphazardly. Do you stop there? Absolutely not!

Once you've tried the immediate ways, you agonize to make it look right on you, the individual. You observe a lot. You think about what you see. You take the time to experiment, trying out the possibilities. You shift the hat around and ask, "How does this look?" Does it make sense if I wear it this way? What if I wear it the way everybody wears it? What if I wear it backwards? What if I wear it inside out? What if I shift it a bit to the right or to the left? What if I keep it straight up?

You think about what might work. You look. You think. You try. You assess. You try again. You do it several ways before you see how it really works for you. Then you make the decisions. When it works you'll know, because it'll feel comfortable and sit just right!

learners, and he started to share his interests with me. He wanted to
be a civil defense worker when he grew up. He had a cache of pamphlets and handouts from the state's Civil Defense Department. He
knew those pamphlets thoroughly, not by reading them (he labored
over many of the words, skipping many of them as he worked his way
through the narrative), but through conversations with others. He
would often call the Director of Civil Defense, who gave him information over the phone. He also had an extensive list of agencies to
contact in case of emergencies resulting from natural disasters.

One day Joshua asked, "How are hurricanes formed?" I told
him I didn't know and asked, "How can we find out?" To find out, we
looked for books. Joshua tried to read the information we found. The
text said that the hurricane's eye could be 5–30 miles across. "What
does *across* mean?" he asked. I was perplexed; *across* didn't seem like a
hard word. Surely, I thought, all fifth graders must know what it
means! I asked Joshua what he thought the word meant. He kept
saying that it was the wind speed of the hurricane's eye. He would not
let go of this thinking. I tried to explain the meaning by having him
look at the crosswalk. I asked him to look at how the markings span
"across" the street. I tried different ways of helping him visualize the
meaning of the word. He held onto his meaning of "wind speed."

As I had been doing all along, I recorded my possible interpretations on my HT sheet (see Example 3). Did Joshua get confused
about the meaning of *across* because he expected one meaning and
got another? Does Joshua expect print/text to make sense? Does
Joshua have effective strategies for making meaning from print? Does
Joshua privilege literal meaning? Does he make connections between
what he reads and what he knows? Is he rigid in his thinking? Will he
take risks as a reader? Consider new possibilities?

I decided to look across all the interpretations I'd made since
I'd started working with Joshua. Doing so allowed me to develop some
hypotheses. I wondered if Joshua did not have a systematic way of
making meaning from print. It seemed almost as if he used what he
could gather from print (a few words here and there) and then
constructed his own meaning, independent of the text (or teachers)!
My curricular decision was to observe his meaning-making processes
more carefully. What strategies was he using?

The following day, Joshua brought in a replica of a hurricane's
eye. He had made it with the cotton from cotton swabs. "This is
fragile," he said protectively. Together, we continued our studies on
weather. In our readings, Joshua came upon the word *precipitation*. He
was very curious about it. We then went to the dictionary to look up
the word. We mapped it so Joshua could visualize the many facets of
the word. He struggled long and hard with the different words used
to tell about the meaning of precipitation. He was particularly inter-

Example 3. The author produced this HT sheet after working with Joshua. *Diane Stephens' commentary is shown in italics.*

Hypothesis-Test Sheet

Name Joshua

Teacher Lynn Yoshizaki

Date _____

Page ___1___ of ___1___

Observations *(Data, Events)*	Interpretations *(What I think)*	Hypotheses *(What will the answer to my questions probably be? Predictions)*	Curricular Decisions *(Experiments)*
After reading *Storms* at home, Joshua came to our Friday session. He talked about hurricanes. When he tried to explain how hurricanes are formed, he forgot for a moment so he referred to the book. He then talked about how the hurricanes are formed. He talked about the "eye" of the hurricane. He talked about why airplanes fly to the eye of the hurricane.	J seemed confident about his knowledge of hurricanes. J knew exactly where to look to regain the information he forgot. J seems to speak/have previous knowledge of hurricanes. J seems to connect meaningfully with print when he is interested.** The reading material was appropriate to J's reading skills.**	Is J's information from his reading? Could it be from other sources? What must the text look like to allow J to understand the material?** Did someone explain how hurricanes are formed to J? Is J making meaning with the print because someone explained it to him before he read this book? If this is so, then is his knowledge gained through the talk? *I think it is interesting to think about how it is that he becomes knowledgeable!*	Check closer to begin to know at what point J begins to comprehend text. *Am not sure how it flows.* Ask J to talk about where/how he gets his information on storms, other than the book. Need to check J's oral reading with his explanations using the text directly.
		**I find this/these particularly interesting. Does this mean that Joshua has the kinds of reading strategies he needs or that he does not use the strategies unless the text is "meaningful"? Or should we slot in "familiar"? Will he use strategies if the text if familiar? Will he only use them if he feels that he already knows something? Does that mean that risk taking/confidence is a factor? Also, just what do we know about his strategies? Does he seem to be a strategic reader? Use his strategies flexibly? Independently? Does he consistently privilege meaning? What are the differences you see between text he cares about (already knows something about) and text he doesn't seem to care about/know about?*	

Afterthought (1/28): Interesting to note that Joshua only focused on hurricanes though the book covers the gamut. Why? Need to investigate further his knowledge of the rest of the material to check if past experiences influenced his understanding rather than actual reading.

Notes

What does one do with the inconsistencies that pop up re: data collected over the past? For example: J seems very verbal and fluid in his retelling; J doesn't seem to connect with print as well. *How* do you look at it?

Mostly it's a matter of just seeing it as data and looking for a frame that explains it all. That way you don't really end up with inconsistencies but a pattern. Oh, I can't get this down in words—let's talk!

If I am so "literal," how do I break out of it?

I don't see you as "literal," just quick to help. You want to help!

J's ability to retell his experiences is tremendous, but the retelling most often has been through "real" experiences.

This idea is fascinating! Where does it take you?

ested in the words *snow* and *blizzards*. He wondered why it didn't snow in Hawaii and what snow looked like. He wanted to know what blizzards were.

The following session we talked about creating some weather conditions. We talked about making a weather chamber. This chamber would simulate rain, snow, and a tornado. I asked Joshua to write down the materials we would need and the instructions for the chamber. I asked him to read back what he wrote. We filled in some missing words to make our directions make sense.

The big day came. Joshua worked with Ashley, another Engagements student. Together they read over the directions. I noticed that when he stumbled over a word, he reread it to correct himself. He worked hard building the chamber. For safety reasons, I made the necessary cuts in the plastic liter bottles, but I had him participate vicariously:

> "Joshua, I'll make the cuts for the chamber. I'm going to eye-ball the cuts."
>
> "What's eye-balling?" he asked, with a bit of a smirk.
>
> "Oh, it's when you guess where you want to make your cuts by just looking and guesstimating. Can you yell stop when you think I've made the cuts long enough?"

The chamber worked beautifully. The steam from the hot water rose to meet the cold air from the dry ice. The simulation created a form of snow, rain, and a tornado. Joshua watched in awe as he saw these natural phenomena happen in a controlled environment. Using what he already knew about hurricanes, Joshua connected the simulation to real weather conditions. He knew about favorable conditions causing weather phenomena. "It's like how hurricanes are formed; warm air rises to meet cold air. It happens over the ocean!" he shouted. The abstraction made sense to him. It seemed he had linked prior knowledge to the new experience in order to make sense of the world and the word. Joshua now owned the word precipitation.

These observations (among others) enabled me to test some of my hypotheses. I became pretty sure that Joshua could make connections from real-world experiences to new words he encountered in his reading. What I didn't understand was under what conditions he would make these connections.

I went back through my prior observations, interpretations, and hypotheses. I began to see a new pattern. It seemed to me that when (1) Joshua was particularly interested in a topic (2) he recognized that he did not know something, *and* (3) he was comfortable enough to take a learning risk, so he did what was necessary to work out the meaning of ideas and words he encountered. This was a pretty complicated set of hypotheses! Again, I decided to observe him some more, in various contexts, to see if the hypotheses were true.

Over the next few weeks, I learned that they were. When Joshua was interested and felt safe but didn't understand, he used his knowledge of the world and from the text to figure things out. When any of these conditions was missing, he did not. He created his own idiosyncratic meaning instead. During this time, I also learned that Joshua had a variety of strategies for making meaning from print (he could use semantic, syntactic, and grapho-phonemic cues), he just didn't use them consistently. When he lacked confidence, he abandoned efficient use of strategies.

When Joshua and I began working with each other, I hadn't known where or how to begin to help without falling into a "fix." I decided to work on the path that seemed most natural to Joshua; I started with his interests. One thing led to another and another and finally to the weather chamber. He ended up demonstrating, proudly and confidently, the weather chamber experiment to the whole class.

As we learned together about weather, I was learning about him. Once I had tested out my hypotheses and was pretty sure I understood that he could make connections and how important it was for him to feel confident, I was able to adjust things in the classroom so that he consistently felt confident enough to take risks. One day, for example, I arranged for him to demonstrate the weather chamber experiment for a group of second graders. As he walked his audience through the procedure, he seemed excited and even joyful. Later, he shared with them his knowledge of hurricanes.

Over time, during group work, Joshua began to read out loud for his classmates. When he came upon a word he couldn't figure out, he would ask for help. This was so public for him but he displayed no insecurities. Joshua's confidence was building with every risk he took.

As Joshua gained in stature and credibility, his reading improved and so did his writing. I could see change happen. In January, he was still writing incomplete sentences in very large letters which spanned the page. As the year progressed, he began writing complete thoughts, and using the smaller printing style of his peers. He was using print to communicate. Earlier in the year, he had copied sentences from the textbook. Over time, he became more independent of the text and wrote his own sentences. He explained, "It takes too long to copy from the book—I'll just write my own." He used picture clues and relied heavily on his prior knowledge to help himself. The changes were fascinating to watch. I thought to myself, this is amazing! This is "learning taking place inside/out!" (Smith, 1988).

I realized that through inquiry, Joshua had reinvented himself as an active, empowered learner. Over time, he became a valued member of our class. He started to share his prized possessions, the

cache of pamphlets and booklets on weather he carried to and from
school daily in a simple brown bag. Classmates flocked to him with
their questions about natural disasters. He organized and headed a
weather news team, giving daily reports. Every day when he gave the
weather report, Joshua wore the broadest grin anyone could imagine.
I felt the warmth radiating from him, his confidence, his energy. He
was elected peer mediator, representing our class.

Once I had believed that I was being helpful to every student
because I knew what children needed to learn in order to read. My
experiences with Joshua changed my thinking. He taught me about
the spirit of inquiry he embodied. His inquiry was to understand
weather, mine was to understand him. Watching him learn (initially in
fifth grade and then again in sixth grade), studying him as a learner,
recording observations, thinking through interpretations, trying out
hypotheses, I started to understand: Attending to a child's individual-
ity is where effective teaching begins.

Watching Joshua change, I understood that missing element I
had searched for. Learning is about making sense of the world. It's
about taking risks. It's about feeling confident. Teaching is about
understanding. It is about being there to nudge, to question, to create
conditions that will support the student as learner. This was the
remedy for the gnawing discomfort: Teaching is about understanding
learners enough to support their learning. HT helped me to focus on
the learning so I could understand enough about it to support it.

I'm not sure just how far the HT way of thinking will take me. I
do know that it has impacted my life, personally and professionally. I
do know I need to keep company with those who continue to read, to
talk, who keep their inquiries alive. HT is about truly watching, truly
listening, truly looking.

Reference   Smith, F. (1988). *Understanding reading: A psycholinguistic analysis of reading
and learning to read.* Hillsdale, NJ: Erlbaum.

Devin

Elaine Tsuchiyama
Waiau Elementary School, Hawaii

Explores how author helped Devin, a first grader, succeed in one-on-one settings but did not know how to help him succeed in classroom setting. Helps reader understand (again) that HT is not a "cure-all" and that understanding a child in a one-on-one situation sometimes leads to hard questions about classroom practices.

From the first day of school, Devin was outgoing and full of energy. My teacher's eyes saw him as a capable but active child, frequently unfocused, who loved to talk with others (to the point that the children found him interfering with their own learning), who seldom finished his assignments. Unlocking the mystery to what was his apparent inability to concentrate and to complete given assignments made Devin my choice for the Engagements project.

About a month before my first one-on-one session with Devin, I recorded some observations of him in the classroom. We were writing farewell letters to the two University of Hawaii teacher education students who had been working in my classroom:

9:25 a.m.	Playing with his pencil
9:26 a.m.	Gerry says, "Start working, Devin." Devin mimics, "Start? Start? . . ."
9:29 a.m.	Finger in mouth and staring outside
9:34 a.m.	Finger still in mouth and staring outside without saying anything
9:36 a.m.	I remind Devin to focus on his assignment
9:39 a.m.	Again seen with finger in mouth and not writing his letter
9:45 a.m.	Recess bell rings. Devin's paper has *Dece* on it, written in large letters
10:00 a.m.	After recess, I do a read aloud. Then I explain to the children what we will be doing for our Christmas project for McDonald's and Foodland. The children who have not completed their two letters are asked to complete them before drawing their Christmas picture.
10:28 a.m.	Devin says the letters of the alphabet out loud as he writes a word

11:15 a.m.   Getting ready for lunch. Devin still has not completed his letters

1:15 p.m.   Finally finishes his second letter

During our parent–teacher conference in November, Devin's mother explained to me that Devin had had difficulty focusing on his class assignments since kindergarten. He showed the same sort of characteristics at home. Because this behavior persisted in first grade, Devin's mom took him to see a child psychiatrist. By listening to her stories and looking at his report card and narrative, the doctor indicated that perhaps Devin had an attention-deficit hyperactivity disorder. His mother agreed that Devin exhibited many characteristics of an ADHD child. Meanwhile, the counselor at our school had given Devin the Slosson Intelligence Test: Devin scored a 129. The counselor was quite surprised; he said he had never seen a child score that high for this age level. Devin's score indicated that he was "knowledgeable" and had "memory retention." The counselor explained that Devin could recite the numbers backwards, a difficult task for many children his age. His mother requested that the district's diagnostic team also test Devin. His scores indicated that he did not qualify for special education services. He did exceptionally well in math reasoning.

It was about this time that the Engagements project began. The first item on my Engagements agenda was establishing a sense of a safe place and developing a warm relationship with Devin. Since this was midway into the school year, it wasn't as though I did not know him. Devin had already experienced my frequent reminders to focus and to complete his assignments, so I felt it was important that this new experience be particularly positive and rewarding. I realized that this first encounter in the new situation was critical. I'd recently read Ralph Peterson's *Life in a Crowded Place* (1992) and was aware of how important rituals, ceremonies, rites, and celebrations were.

We met in the cafeteria—not really the best place to set up "shop," but with four other children also participating in Engagements, the only place available at the school. As we entered the cafeteria, I asked Devin to choose a place to sit. It was not an easy decision because the area was so spacious, but he soon found a spot. (This became a ritual for Devin: each time, he decided where we would sit.) I said that I had brought in alligator books because he had said he wanted to learn about alligators. I'd also brought in other animal books because he'd expressed interest in them, too. I started with the story *Alligator's Toothache* (DeGroat, 1977), a wordless book— but this particular story did not interest him. So we looked at a nonfiction book about alligators and crocodiles. He conversed as we looked at the pictures. Occasionally Devin asked me to read what particular pictures were about. He then became quite interested in the fish book. He was interacting with what he saw in the books and engaging in a conversation with me about the books. I asked him to draw his favorite fish. As he drew the Australian lung fish, Devin explained, "These are the scales, nose, eyes." I said, "Nose? Do lung fish have noses?"

This was a learning experience for me because I was practicing being less judgmental, having him be the teacher and me the learner. I consciously tried not to lead Devin to discover what *I* wanted him to discover. Do you know how difficult this can be? I taxed my listening skills, listening to what he was saying and using this information as a way of sustaining curiosity. I realized that we teachers expect children to listen to us attentively, but we often do not practice this. I often have so much on my mind that I neglect to focus on what the child is telling me through words and actions.

For the Engagements project, Diane Stephens asked us to try filling out an HT sheet for each student. My initial observations about Devin included comments like, "Focused on the books shared with me the whole time except for the wordless book" and "Related experience in reference to alligators." For each of these, I generated at least five interpretations. For each observation, I also developed a hypothesis and a curricular decision. I was beginning to learn about HT.

When Diane responded to this HT sheet, she noted that my interpretations were great but that my hypotheses ("Works better in a one-to-one situation") were more like conclusions than something to test out. My curricular decisions ("Needs to stay away from the mainstream of other children") seemed like "*the* fix" or "*the* answer" rather than a way to figure out if my hypotheses were true or not. My observations read more like judgments than things I noticed. My quest, Diane reminded me, was to discover reasons for behaviors. Once I was "pretty sure" I understood Devin's behaviors, then—and only then— would I be able to make informed curricular decisions that would benefit Devin as a learner.

Acting like a scientist and making insightful observations, interpretations, hypotheses, and curricular decisions was extremely difficult for me. As a teacher, I had learned to make quick decisions. Diane expected me to use the HT process to slow down my thinking process, to be extremely reflective in my decision making. This was not an easy thing to do.

The HT process continued to challenge me. Diane's comments over the next several weeks were extremely helpful. With the HT process, it became clear to me that as teachers we often box ourselves into thinking that there are only *X* number of possibilities and use common strategies such as flash cards, writing, and drawing as curricular decisions, rather than supporting the child by pushing our own thinking and trying to understand the child. We focus instead on fixing the child's problem.

In subsequent engagement times, Devin and I continued to focus on what Devin wanted to explore: alligators, crocodiles, and cats. He was in charge of the learning. As an extension of his interest in alligators we made "alligator" cookies with corn flakes. He wanted to make the cookies so all of his classmates could eat them. Sharing them with the class was a great idea—Devin beamed!

During our fourth session, I read *Devin and Goliath* (Christian, 1974). I specifically chose this book because I wanted Devin to connect books and stories with his name and himself. Goliath was a turtle. As it turned out, Devin had already heard this story in kindergarten, so his interest was not as keen as I had hoped. When I asked him to write about the story, he asked me to write his thoughts down for him. Writing did not seem to be a joyful endeavor for Devin. He seemed to prefer avoiding it. I next asked if he would like to visit the school's science room to look at the turtles. He was receptive to this idea. While we watched the turtle, I wrote down a number of the comments he made:

> The turtle can climb on the rock.
> There are three same kinds of turtles.
> There are orange strip things on the cheeks.
> It swims.
> He's paddling.
> He is looking at me.
> He is swimming slowly. That big turtle is over way down here and this turtle over here is so little.
> Has food inside for the turtle to eat—the orange stuff.
> To play with too, I think.
> He couldn't breathe underwater. He has to come up sometimes.
> His head is coming out of the water. It can stay still sometimes. It looks at my Kleenex. [Devin had a cold that day.]

I found it delightful when he exclaimed, "How come he [the turtle] likes to look at me? It must be Devin, that's why." At our next session, Devin wanted me to read the turtle books. He liked *Devin and Goliath* better this time. We went to the science room to bring some turtles to leave in our classroom, so Devin's classmates could view them. I asked Devin to make a warning sign, so the children would not touch them. He dictated what he wanted to say. I, in turn, recorded the message on paper and then asked him to recopy it neatly on construction paper to put with our turtle exhibit. He did an excellent job of recopying. He was amazed that he had copied the message so quickly. He wrote, "See our turtles. Please do not touch because they will bite." As he copied, Devin said the letters out loud. He needed to look often at the dictation—look, write, look, write.

Based on my observations, I brainstormed interpretations: "Does Devin function differently when given control or not given control of the situation?" "How does his mind think?" "How much information does Devin process?" "Under what conditions does the inquiry shut down and under what conditions does he open up again?" "If he's a strong oral communicator, why doesn't he transfer that into his reading and writing?" (Example 4 shows several weeks' worth of HT sheets.)

By the beginning of February, I was convinced that the HT process was worthwhile—but frustrating. First, it took time to reflect on what happened, then generate interpretations, come up with a hypothesis, and make curricular decisions. After working with the children in the classroom all day, I found myself too exhausted to think about what Devin did during our special time together. This was something I needed to work out for myself. Second, I found that although I had taught for over twenty years, my observation skills were poor. I had learned to form generalities and make quick decisions, but I had not honed the skill of looking more closely at what actually transpired between the child and me. I had not developed myself as an effective "kidwatcher" (Goodman, 1986) or the ability to look at the children as my curricular informants (Short, Harste, & Burke, 1996).

During the sixth session, Diane spent some time sitting with Devin and me. We shared with her some things we had found out about where alligators lived. A lengthy discussion followed, as Diane probed what Devin was thinking. Although Devin and I had talked about where alligators were found, he explained to Diane (incorrectly) that alligators could be found in the ocean. Devin said that if Diane were swimming in the ocean, she could be bitten by an alligator. Since this did not match our earlier conclusion, Diane asked Devin how he could find out for sure what kind of water alligators lived in. He immediately replied, "Go to the library." Diane suggested that Devin write that down, and he did, without hesitation. I cried when I saw this; I was so overjoyed by this accomplishment. He had not written that quickly or easily all year! Prior to this, he'd used no vowels in his writings, but this time the word "library" was written *libre*. When I later explained to him why I cried, he said that his mom did the same one time. He also said it was his birthday present to me because it was my birthday.

Looking across what had happened that day and on earlier days, I began to form a hypothesis:

> If Devin is interested in what is being presented, then he can be focused for a long period of time.

I wrote this on my HT sheet, and next to it wrote this curricular decision (CD):

> Teach concepts through topics that interest him.

Diane wrote in the margin next to this CD:

> You are closing things down too quickly. Your "H" is that you wonder if interest is a factor, then you seem to conclude that it is and then right away try to fix it by bringing in things you think will interest him.

Instead I needed to test hypothesis. I could do this by observing Devin at various points during the day. When was he focused? When was he not focused? What were the characteristics of those tasks? Did he seem more interested in some than others? Was there a relationship between when he was focused (or not) and his level of interest? I began to make these observations in the classroom.

Meanwhile, in our one-on-one sessions, Devin continued to be hooked on ocean books. He was quite interested in looking at *Find Demi's Sea Creatures* (Demi, 1991) which has a format similar to *Where's Waldo?* (Handford, 1987). He could find many of the hidden animals, and he seemed to be enjoying our time together.

Two weeks later, Devin shared with Elaine Yoshioka (district language arts resource teacher) and Diane the books we had brought to the cafeteria. He explained to them which books he had chosen and which ones I had chosen. Devin started his exploration with them by looking at *Monsters of the Sea* (Gelman, 1990). As he scanned the pictures in this book, the jellyfish seemed to intrigue him. He then turned to *Beneath the Waves* (Wu, 1992) which also had information about jellyfish. He intently studied the pictures. He asked me which jellyfish I liked; I said, "the giant one" and he responded with "I like that one, too." The jellyfish was purple and I said that purple was my favorite color. He then said that purple was his favorite color, too.

He studied the picture of the giant jellyfish with a diver next to it. Diane asked, "Devin, how long do you think the giant jellyfish is?" She continued, "Let's pretend that these backpacks are the head. Use this paper and show me where you would place it on the table to show how long the jellyfish is." To figure this out, Devin asked me to lie on the cafeteria table's bench to help him visualize the length of the diver. Devin placed the book next to me (the diver), doing this several times. He seemed intent on figuring out how long this giant jellyfish was.

Devin began using his fingers to measure. He said, "One feet, two feet . . ." until he counted to "eleven feet." Each span he measured actually seemed approximately a foot in length. Did he know how much a foot was?

Example 4. Several weeks' worth of the author's HT sheets about Devin. *Diane Stephens' commentary is shown in italics.*

Hypothesis-Test Sheet

Name: Devin

Teacher: Elaine Tsuchiyama

Date: Feb. 10

Page 1 of 2

"Starting with" Hypotheses

"Starting with" Hypotheses	Curricular Decisions
Does having a stake in the learning experience help Devin to make meaningful connections?	
If interested in the topic, Devin is focused and not distracted. Does interest in the topic correlate directly with attention span?	Find out as much as possible through conversation what he likes/is interested in. "I wonder about . . ."
If Devin feels comfortable and not threatened, then Devin is focused. Is "comfortability" an important factor that drives Devin to learn or not learn?	Create a safe place—speak in soft tone, be less judgmental.
If topic of study is self-initiated, then Devin is focused. Do self-initiated activities make Devin become focused and increase attention span—sustained interest on the task at hand?	
If there are no distractions around him, then Devin is focused on the assignment at hand.	Have Devin situate himself in the classroom whereby he is not facing the whole class.
If he feels special, then he is focused.	Continue to nurture IALAC in the classroom.
If no set expectations are placed upon him, then he is focused and wants to get involved.	

These hypotheses are GREAT! Now you need to figure out how to test them out (instead of acting on them as if they are true).

Date: Feb. 25   Session: #12

Observations	Interpretations	Hypotheses	Curricular Decisions
Seemed to enjoy kinesthetic experience of measuring out what 100 feet looked like using nonstandard measure of using his own feet.	"Doing" physically makes understanding concrete for Devin. Likes to move around. Needs to move around when learning. Interested in finding out for himself.	Is Devin a "kinesthetic learner"?	Make careful observations to see when Devin engages in the assignment.
Seemed to understand some of the ideas Diane was sharing about putting large animals to scale in books.	Likes Diane. Complex ideas can be understood by Devin—ready to learn about drawings put to scale. Smart, matured thinker. Ready to learn. Important for him to understand.	Does Devin like to be challenged with complex ideas?	Note how he responds during discussions.

Observations	Interpretations	Hypotheses	
Continues to be intrigued by the jellyfish	Needs to exhaust all possibilities before finding another topic of interest Loves the idea of "giantness" Loves sea creatures in general Unusual things attract his attention Loves to learn when topic is of interest to him	Is Devin a learner that learns for depth? Does he need to satisfy his own curiosity before he is ready to move on to another topic? Does he need more time to process information?	
Focused on one topic for one hour	Oral communication is his strength Written work not expected of him Loves challenges Has a stake in the thinking—to further his own interest Relaxed—no timeframe to finish	Devin is a thinker.	
		These seem to be quite strong—that is generative. I am not sure, though, that the label "kinesthetic" will be particularly helpful. Most of us need to "see" the complex in our mind. The pacing is just one way Devin does this. What seems to matter here is that he works hard to make meaning.	

Date: March 1		Session: #13	
Observations	**Interpretations**	**Hypotheses**	**Curricular Decisions**
Wrote a sentence by himself about the jellyfish.	Beginning to feel more comfortable forming letters of the alphabet. More familiar with words. Able to hear sounds in words and reproduce them on paper. ** Something he wants to write about. Doesn't view writing as difficult as before.	Is Devin beginning to view himself as a writer?	Continue to monitor amount of text Devin writes.
Says each word aloud as he writes.	Needs to hear first to confirm spelling. Just his "style" of writing. Wants to have what is being written make sense. ** Conscious that he can't just write any letters—knows that sounds are related to letters of the alphabet. **	Does Devin need to *hear* what he's thinking to process meaning?	
Devin "wasn't too excited."	Actually finds writing too difficult. Writing sounds too "schoolish." Not ready to write. Hasn't felt the power of what words can do. Wants to keep learning experiences on personal level.		*Your interpretations here are strong. I find myself, however, going in a slightly different direction with the hypotheses. My mind said things like "Understands print-to-speech connection?" "Spells like it sounds?" "Is planful/strategic as writer?" Which means that I might have brought forward as hypotheses the interpretations I marked with asterisks. I would also suggest you explore if Devin uses his sound–symbol knowledge when he reads.*

Example 4. Continued

When Diane asked if he was sure the length was eleven feet, he again measured the same way. This time he counted thirteen feet. Devin said this time it was longer because the first time he measured only the tentacles and the second time he measured from the top of the head. Diane then asked him how long the head was. He again used his fingers and said that it was one foot. But he revised his response by measuring again and saying that it was two feet. (I wondered how he had figured out how long the head was—had he used subtraction?) He asked Diane to write down "11 feet and 13 feet if you add the head" on a piece of paper, which she did.

Devin also wanted to record that the head was two feet long and asked Diane to write that on the paper. Instead, she asked him to write it, and so he did. He knew how to spell *the*. As he wrote "head," he said the word out loud. He wrote *ha*, stopped a while, and then added another *a* and then a *d*. He wrote *s* for "was," then self-corrected and put a *w* in front of it. His writing (see Figure 3) again astounded me.

To top the day off, my student teacher told me that after returning to the classroom, Devin came to her and said, "Do you want to know about jellyfish?" She said the way he said it made her laugh, and she could not say no. His facial expression got her hooked, even though she would have normally said no because she was working with another child. Devin then began telling her that the jellyfish was thirteen feet long and that it turns into a glob when it is out of the water. She invited him to share what he'd learned with the class after first recess. They used the ruler to measure out thirteen feet.

This "critical incident" (Newman, 1992) was phenomenal because it helped me understand that Devin was a highly intelligent youngster. He could think with depth, verify his thinking, and explain his thought process to others. I hadn't been able to "see" this Devin in the classroom. I began to wonder what kinds of curricular changes I would need to make so that Devin could have this kind of success in the classroom.

During our eleventh session, Devin again opened *Beneath the Waves* (Wu, 1992). He continued to be intrigued by the picture of the jellyfish. He said he wanted to know more about the giant jellyfish because "it's the most beautiful one in the whole wide world." He continued to scan the book. Upon coming to the wolf eel, he said, "I don't like the wolf eel because it eats my favorite thing." (The wolf eel was eating the sea urchin.) Then he said, "You would like this [a small orange fish] because you like pretty things." I was touched and surprised by this. He obviously had been paying more attention in the classroom than I had given him credit for.

Hereafter, jellyfish captivated him. I decided that in the classroom I would find beginning reader books that had to do with the ocean and have him pair off with a friend to read them together. I'd become pretty sure that Devin needed someone he could share his thoughts with, and that talking seemed to be an integral part of his learning process. Although Devin avoided writing in a whole-group setting, he was willing to dictate stories. One day he dictated this story to my student teacher:

> Once there was a jellyfish. He lived in the pond. He swam in the rocks. He climbed on the rocks. He stung fish in the water, and he ate them.

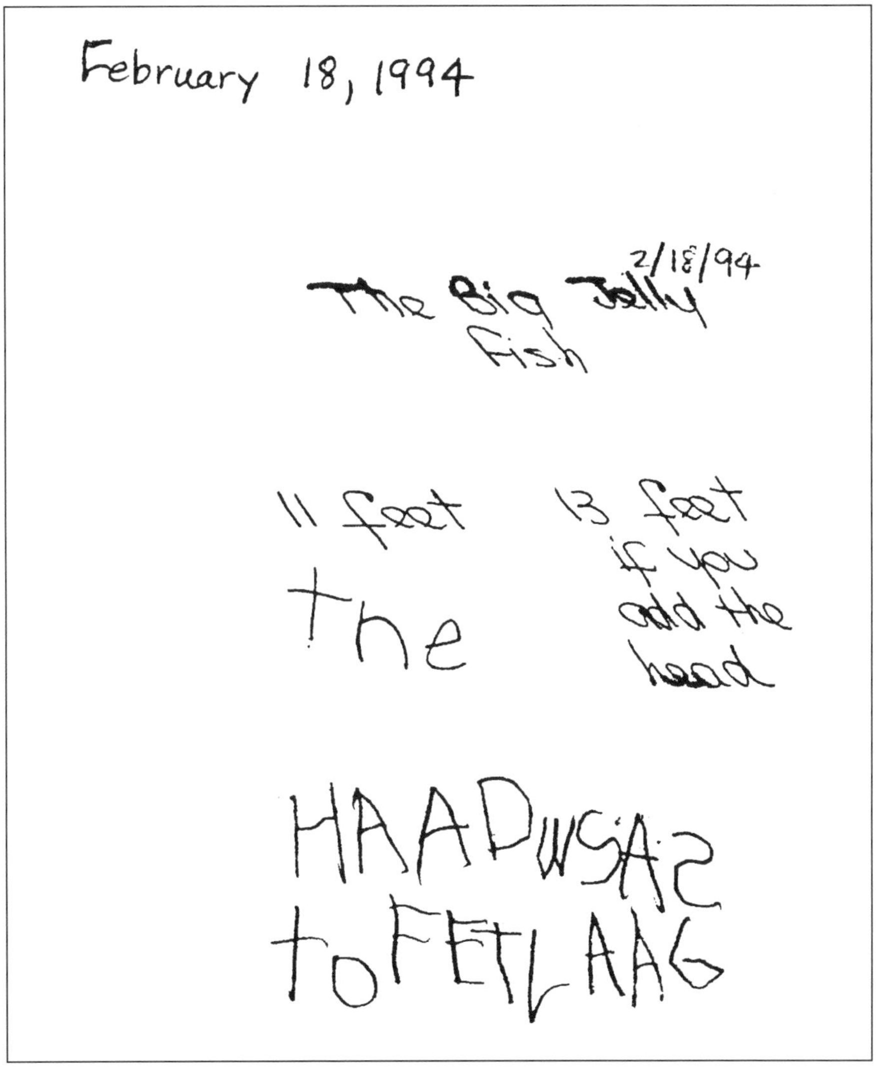

Figure 3.
Devin recorded his observations about how long the jellyfish's head was.

The jellyfish couldn't talk, but Devin wishes he could talk.
He climbed on the sand, and he ate his fish over there. He loved to sit on his favorite rock. He loved to swim in his favorite pond. The pond had clean water, and it feeled good in there.

On March 28, our nineteenth session together, Devin surprised me by excitedly pulling out "jellyfish" from his backpack: two made with towels and strings and one made with a plastic cap. Devin—the "unfocused" child who "had trouble finishing assignments," who had been labeled ADHD—had spent spring break the week before making three jellyfish *on his own,* using towels, strings, a piece of plastic, and a plastic cap! His smile was contagious. In this instance, Devin washed away my day-to-day stress of teaching—children not listening, children having difficulty grasping concepts, children showing disrespect to themselves and others, irate parents, report cards, an abundance of meetings and reports to tend to—*this* was teaching and learning at its best.

Throughout the twenty sessions we spent together, Devin showed an incredible ability to focus on what he was studying. Over those sessions, using the HT process, I became pretty sure that choice and interest were major factors. Not once did he waver. In these sessions, Devin most definitely did not look like a child with an attention-deficit disorder!

Having no set agenda or expectations also seemed to motivate Devin to learn. When he could work at his own pace, learning seemed natural and meaningful, and he seemed to feel safe and comfortable. He seemed to need ample space to think and explore. He was able to make connections with what he heard and saw in books. Devin continued to be a risk taker and ventured out with hypotheses of his own to explain things about alligators and jellyfish. He wrote when it served some function for him.

In our one-on-one sessions, Devin showed me what teaching is all about: the engagements that the learner makes which leave lasting effects on that person and those around him or her. Devin made jellyfish during the spring break because he wanted to. He shared information with his classmates because he loved what he had learned. By exploring these topics Devin invited me into his thinking, allowing me to see the world from his perspective. These stories helped me gain new insights into Devin as a person, as a learner.

But I still worried about him in my classroom. In our one-on-one sessions, he sometimes seemed to need to exhaust all possibilities before going on to the next main idea. The way my classroom was structured, this was not possible. There, he needed to be able to shift his focus from topic to topic, based on the way I had organized the day. In my classroom, his intense interest in one topic became a handicap. Also, both in the one-on-one times and in the large-group setting, he was willing to write only when it served some immediate function for him. However, in the classroom, children did not always personally value the writing I asked them to do. One day, for example, I thought that giving him a "bare book" for his jellyfish story would motivate him to copy what he had dictated. I wanted him to copy it, but he was not interested. Copying it over served no function for him.

I ended that semester, knowing more and knowing less. I understood more about Devin as a learner; I understood more about how to help him in a one-on-one setting—but I had new questions about how to help him, and others like him, in the classroom.

References

Christian, M. (1974). *Devin and Goliath.* Reading, MA: Addison Wesley.

DeGroat, D. (1977). *Alligator's toothache.* New York: Crown.

Demi. (1991). *Find Demi's sea creatures: An animal game book.* New York: Putman and Grosser.

Gelman, R.G. (1990). *Monsters of the sea.* Boston, MA: Little, Brown, and Company.

Goodman, K. (1986). *What's whole in whole language?* Richmond Hill, Ontario: Scholastic.

Handford, M. (1987). *Where's Waldo?* Boston, MA: Little, Brown, and Company.

Newman, J. (1992). *Finding your own way: Teachers explore their assumptions.* Portsmouth, NH: Heinemann.

Peterson, R. (1992). *Life in a crowded place: Making a learning community.* Portsmouth, NH: Heinemann.

Short, K., Harste, J.C., & Burke, C. (1996). *Creating classrooms for authors and inquirers.* Portsmouth, NH: Heinemann.

Wu, N. (1992). *Beneath the waves: Exploring the hidden world of the kelp forest.* San Francisco: Chronicle.

Mayra

Diane Parker
Waikele Elementary School, Hawaii

Illustrates how Mayra transformed herself in grades four through six. Shows the HT collaborative conversation, via the author's exchange of letters with Diane Stephens.

August 22

[From Diane Stephens' first letter to class.] Welcome to this class. I have been teaching assessment classes for a long time now and look forward to the experience. I worry a lot about kids who are not experiencing school success because they struggle with reading. I see assessment courses as a way to help you help them.

In this course, we will work collaboratively to understand children from your classroom you are worried about. Real inquiry, not given assignments, will determine what you read; you will read to answer your own questions. There will only be one major requirement: To do the very best you can do to understand one child as reader.

I look forward to getting to know all of you and to our learning together this semester.

September 20

I hope you don't mind my using a letter format for our written conversations. I've found it personalizes the writing more for me. In fact, I've extended the concept to my students, inviting them to write their learning log entries as letters to me, and I've found they had much more to say.

Let me start our dialogue by giving you a little more information about the child I'm working with, where I am in my never-ending quest to understand learning and learners, and how these things are connected.

Mayra came from the Philippines in the middle of her kindergarten year. Because she had had no formal schooling and spoke no English yet, her kindergarten teacher retained her so she had another full year of kindergarten. She entered my class as a first grader, and I had the good fortune to keep her through both her first- and second-grade years. She is now in fourth grade and in the "low" reading

---

Throughout this dialogic chapter, we have used different typefaces to denote the individual speakers. Excerpts from Diane Stephens' letters to the author are printed in this type. Excerpts from the author's letters to Diane are printed in this way.

group in her homogeneously grouped class. She has also been sent to a pullout ESL program since beginning third grade.

I had begun exploring constructivism and mathematics education when Mayra was my student and I became especially interested in her as a learner. I've been studying her mathematics learning quite closely, even through her third-grade year. She would come to ask me for help, although she was by then in a different class.

Mayra has a wonderful desire to learn, and she drives herself to try to make sense of everything around her. As she puts it, "I'm very curious. I'm always asking, 'Why?'" The thinking she demonstrates often astounds me. I believe without a doubt that she is a truly gifted student. I worry about her a lot, though, because she has not scored well on standardized tests, and I am afraid she will be one of those students who falls through the cracks and doesn't get the learning opportunities she should have. That's why I'm especially glad to be working with her.

When Mayra was in my class she was a hesitant and rather reluctant reader, but I always felt it was because of her unfamiliarity with the grammatical structures of English, and that time and immersion would take care of it. But I don't think I knew how to look much more closely than that. It's funny, because I've been working for the past two years to try to understand her as a mathematics learner, yet I don't think I really understand her as a reader.

Because I have come to view learning as a unified whole with similar processes regardless of content, I believe it's theoretically possible for Mayra to learn to use her considerable strengths as a mathematical thinker and problem solver in order to become an equally skillful reader. I want to explore these connections with her and use them to help her.

At our first session yesterday, after some initial talking and book browsing, I did a reading and writing interview with her. Here are some of the questions and her answers (I italicized many of Mayra's answers because I find in them a curious paradox):

1. What is reading?
   It's a class that teaches you how to read, like when you tell the story from a book.

2. Do you think you are a good reader? Why or why not?
   Not that much, because I still can't. *Well, I can read it—I know the meaning, but I can't explain it, and sometimes I don't know the word.*

3. How did you learn to read? Who helped you? How?
   All my teachers helped teach me how to pronounce words and letters.

4. When you are reading, what kinds of problems do you have? What do you do about them?

     I ask my classmate that's near me. If they don't know, I ask my teacher or I look in the dictionary. I read better than the person next to me, so sometimes I help her.

5. Do you like to read? Why or why not?

     Sometimes I like to read, when it's raining. I don't like to read when it's sunny.

6. What is writing?

     When you do something with your pencil and paper. You make a story on it or make letters and numbers.

7. Do you think you are a good writer? Why or why not?

     Yes, because I don't get hard time like reading or math. It's easy to do.

8. How did you learn to write? Who helped you? How?

     For each grade I had a teacher and all of them helped. My mom helped but when I was not in school yet. She held my hand and put the pencil in and moved my hand.

9. Who is a good writer that you know? What makes him or her a good writer?

     Marjorie. She writes neat. She doesn't keep erasing words. She knows what to write. She thinks about what she's going to write before she writes it.

10. When you are writing, what kinds of problems do you have? What do you do about them?

     When I write cursive, I have trouble with b, q, k, and i. Sometimes I don't know what to write in my journal. Then I think about yesterday and what I want to do today. Sometimes a book gives you information or ideas. You could open it and imagine.

11. If you knew that someone was having trouble writing, how would you help them?

     I would help them the same way as the person who helped me. *I'd teach them how to hold the pencil and write letters.*

12. Do you like to write? Why or why not?

     Yes . . . I don't know. Before I didn't but when I began to write for the first day, I wrote one whole page. *I like to write stories.*

Her definitions and comments concerning reading and writing seem to be coming from two different perspectives. I think this is something I need to explore further. I'll try to think it through on my HT sheet (as seen in Example 5).

Example 5. One of the author's initial HT sheets about Mayra.

Hypothesis-Test Sheet

Name _____ Mayra _____

Teacher _____ Diane Parker _____

Date _____ Sept. 19 _____

Page _____ of _____

Observations	Interpretations	Hypotheses	Curricular Decisions
Her definition of reading includes such comments as "telling the story from a book," "pronouncing words and letters," "knowing the meaning," and "knowing the word."	1. Is she caught between two para-digms as a result of her school experiences over the past few years?	Maybe she is worried about her ability to function as a reader based on the views to which she is currently exposed.	Continue to emphasize reading for meaning, with the goal of helping her develop confidence in her ability to do so (and strategies to accomplish this).
	2. Is she not sure which is the "right" paradigm, and therefore she's testing both?		*Revised 9/29 after discussing with Diane:* Try various reading situations (such as shared and independent reading of assigned and self-selected texts, some with pictures and some without); watch and question her to try to determine under what conditions she seems to see herself as an effective reader (or if there are *any* conditions under which she does so).
Her comments about writing include such phrases as "make a story," "make letters and numbers," "holding the pencil," and "you could imagine" (getting ideas from a book).	3. Is she becoming confused about the discrepancy between her own thought processes and what the "system" tells her about her ability?		
	4. Is she beginning to compare herself with others, based on a traditional paradigm?		
	5. Is she still holding on to the idea of reading for meaning in spite of current pressures in the opposite direction (reading to "get the words")?		

We continued with a game and then moved to her topic of current interest, magic. She wants to be able to learn and perform magic tricks, so we are starting there. We found some books on magic and she selected the one she wanted to read first. I thought the text looked a little difficult, but since she had chosen the book I didn't say anything. After she glanced through several pages, she decided to begin with a trick called "The Amazing Magic Box." We discussed the illustrations and talked about what might be involved in preparing the trick. I thought it looked rather complex but again I didn't say anything; I just asked her to read the paragraph describing the trick.

Her reading amazed me! She missed only one or two words, self-corrected many, and nearly all her miscues seemed contextually appropriate. She was also able to explain the paragraph in her own words quite easily. So I am left with a most puzzling question: How can a child, who is considered by traditional measures to be a "poor" reader, read and retell a passage that seems so much more difficult than her usual reading material? (See Example 6.)

September 26   First, I found it fascinating to think about the fact that you said you had been coming to know Mayra as a mathematical thinker but not as a reader. I too am coming at this from a constructivist perspective and suspect that when you change your lens from math to reading you will see many similarities. In part, my understanding of constructivist approaches comes from semiotics, which argues that all meaning is a construction. It might be interesting to make a list of what you understand about Mayra as a learner of mathematics and move from that to hypotheses you might want to explore with her about reading. (On the other hand, I can see reasons why you wouldn't want to do that and would rather gather observations now and look for parallels later.)

Second, you say that you feel she is gifted but worry because she has not scored well on standardized tests. Have you played around with that discrepancy and come up with any ideas (Interpretations) about why that might be?

I also found it interesting that you went from reading, to questions about math, to math. I have seen that happen in the field more generally. A number of people in the language field have been asking questions about math. I think it's great and that the many, many questions serve to move us all towards a constructivist curriculum which I think is a direction that will well serve learners.

Now to your interview: My reactions were similar to yours, although I also saw some overlap (e.g., your interpretations: Mayra may think that reading is getting the words and that what matters about writing is that it should be neat). It's as if she has pieces of a constructivist notion about the writing, but transmission and produc-

Example 6. The author used this HT sheet to try to understand Mayra's successful reading of complex text.

Hypothesis-Test Sheet

Name ___ Mayra ___

Teacher ___ Diane Parker ___

Date ___ Sept. 26 ___

Page ___ of ___

Observations	Interpretations	Hypotheses	Curricular Decisions
She was able to read and explain a series of paragraphs and directions that seem more difficult than her usual (classroom) reading material.	1. Did her motivation and interest in the subject help her? 2. Did the illustrations help her? 3. Is she really a "better" reader than she seems according to traditional measures? 4. Did a safe, risk-free environment allow her to do this? 5. Because this was a "fun" situation to her, did she not think of herself as a poor reader, thereby not being hampered by a possible lack of confidence? 6. Did the context help her? 7. Did the fact that it was a "hands-on" activity help her?	Maybe a combination of motivation and supportive environment enable her to function more effectively as a reader.	Continue to try various reading situations, exploring the possible conditions needed for her to function more effectively as a reader. Also, *ask* her to compare this situation (today's session) with her classroom reading situations, and to reflect on the possible similarities and differences. Try to make sense of this *with her.*

tion notions as well. In the reading, a constructivist notion seems absent. But like you say, let's leave that for the HT sheet.

I have now read and reread the paragraph that Mayra read so well. And I find myself in the same place as you report yourself being. She certainly does not read like someone who is having trouble as a reader! It's also interesting to note that what she told you about herself as reader does not seem to match with what she does as reader. What sense do you make of her reading about the magic box?

September 27   Yes, I did think about making a list of what I understand about Mayra as a mathematics learner and then seeing if there are parallels with my observations of her as a reader. I hesitated because I didn't want to go into her reading with too many preconceived notions. I suppose, though, that much of that list is already in my mind and that I sort of expect to see some of her mathematics strengths play a part in her reading. On the other hand, maybe I won't see them, and then I will have to try to figure out how to help her become more aware of these strengths and to figure out with her how she might apply them to her reading.

You asked me if I have any thoughts/ideas/possible explanations about why she does not score well on standardized tests. Yes, I do. Here are a few of my interpretations:

1. Some of the grammatical structures of English are not a part of her everyday usage, either at school or at home. Being an ESL student, she is also not familiar with many idioms used in English. Standardized tests rely heavily on testing these decontextualized bits and pieces of language.

2. She works slowly and thoroughly, thinking problems through very deliberately and carefully. Standardized tests reward those who can make quick guesses without putting much thought into them. She would probably find it totally against her nature to work like that.

3. She is such a creative thinker that she tends to consider many possible interpretations of questions or situations. Her thinking goes way beyond the "one right answer" mentality.

4. Along with that, she questions everything, not accepting things at face value. I can almost see her looking at those test questions and asking, "Why?" when they don't seem to make sense—as is the case with many of them.

As for what sense I make of her reading that complex magic trick passage and supposedly being a poor reader, I have to admit that I don't make sense of it yet! I've decided to ask *her* to help me make sense of it.

Well, that brings me to this week. We worked for a long time on constructing the magic box. She read and followed the directions, making her own adaptations that she thought would work well (and they did). Then we started a new book, *Mike's Mystery* (Warner, 1988), one of the Boxcar Children stories, which she's loved since we read several when she was in second grade.

We talked a little about what we both remembered of the characters and their previous adventures. We read the blurb on the back cover and she was eager to start reading the book. She began reading the first chapter, reading very slowly and pointing to the words as she read. We only got through two pages. Some words were not familiar to her and she asked about their meaning. Some of her miscues seemed not to affect the meaning of the story ("field" for *fields*) and others were non-words ("nobbed" for *nodded*). She read "lauded" for *laughed*, but self-corrected later. She retold the section without much detail and I couldn't get her to elaborate more. Maybe there wasn't enough text yet to help her. I'll see what happens as we read more.

I want to tell you that I really appreciate your genuine interest in all your students (and in *our* students) and the thoroughness with which you respond to our letters. I know how much time that takes! But you have a great way of pushing our thinking! I'd like to know more about semiotics. I've only heard the term but I don't have any knowledge about it.

October 2   I woke up today thinking about reading and math and semiotics. I don't talk much about semiotics, mostly because it seems a fairly complicated thing and bigger than words. I do have some great materials and I'll be glad to dig them up and share. I think you will find them interesting reading.

Basically, though, semiotics is a belief system, coming out of philosophy, about knowledge and knowing. Semioticians would argue that knowledge is created in transaction. They would also argue that we can never know anything directly.

The process of making meaning from signs is how knowledge is constructed. Peirce, the semiotician who I studied the most, argues that there are but three things/entities; firsts, seconds, and thirds. Firsts are qualities, essences, and can only be known in comparison. Redness, for example, exists but can not come into awareness until it is juxtaposed with something that is not quite the same ("not red"). Once redness has been perceived, it is a second—that is, something perceived in relationship. (All "objects," by the way, "have" these characteristics. That is, firstness is always embedded in secondness and secondness in thirdness.)

So, a first is a quality and a second is perception. Thirds, however, make it possible to build new knowledge because they are the rule or relationship. So redness exists (a first) and we notice it (perception) and we name it. This allows us to construct still other knowledge, e.g., about color.

What all this means is that things can only be known in relationship, and naming makes new learning possible. One needs to know /red/, that is, the rule that distinguishes red from all other colors, in order to build on that knowledge.

In terms of reading and math, their conventional symbols serve as things to be known—which Peirce and other semioticians call "signs." Similarly, the book itself is a sign. We gain understandings from having perceived these signs and formed rules, e.g., we learn /red/, /relationship/, /predictability/. These are all thirds and are logical concepts, arrived at through induction, deduction, and abduction. It is how we know our world.

Knowing is what is central here. We are constructing meaning so we can know our world. In your study of Mayra's thinking, it seems you were looking at how she built her knowledge in one particular category of things to be known. In reading, we look at how she builds her knowledge in another category. Details may vary but the process should be the same—we are studying her process of knowledge construction.

I agree with you that writing down what you know might have narrowed your thinking. I also agree that what you know is already in your head and so it narrows it anyway. (Another idea from semiotics: You can only know those things that have some similarity to something else. This indeed is what allows perception. If things are too dissimilar, we do not juxtapose and so do not "see." Ditto for being too similar.)

I went into reading, by the way, at the doctoral level, because I saw reading as a way to "see" how other people constructed meaning. I also cared a lot about children who were not experiencing school success and had noticed how often that was connected to reading difficulties.

But now, back to Mayra:

Thanks for your thoughtful list of interpretations related to how she scores on standardized tests. In many ways, it seems that she needs to understand that tests are not about thinking. On the other hand, I find myself wondering if her thinking may be too divergent. I expect that some of our brightest and most creative people would have not scored well on standardized tests. Right now, though, the scores are so powerful and kids get hurt by them. If it's possible to teach her about tests so they don't hurt her, that seems a reasonable thing to do—part of helping her take good care of herself.

I read through what you wrote about Mayra's reading and found myself thinking along with you. I was really surprised by the difficulty she had with the text. Somehow I hadn't expected that. I find I am really intrigued now and want to understand what is going on inside her head.

October 3   I was fascinated by your discussion of semiotics (yes, I'd be interested in the readings you mentioned) and I think I see strong theoretical links between semiotics and constructivism. Constructivism argues that learners construct knowledge through reflective abstraction from their own mental action of putting things into relationships. Some radical constructivists in mathematics go so far as to question whether mathematical content exists apart from the individual. They argue that learning and, therefore, mathematical cognition, are dependent on each person's own construction and thus they question whether there is even any mathematics content "out there" to discover!

I see in your description of Peirce's theories what appear to be parallels with some of the things I've been reading about mathematics, but I am still not clear about specific points. For example, Kamii (1990), whose work is based on Piaget's theories, describes three kinds of knowledge which lead to construction from within. The first is physical knowledge, or knowledge of objects in external reality. No cognition is involved here, just sensory, or empirical knowledge—perhaps like Peirce's firsts, such as redness? The second is logico-mathematical knowledge, which consists of relationships created by each individual. An example might be creating an understanding of redness as different from blueness—perhaps Peirce's seconds? This differs from physical knowledge because the source is in the individual's head, not external.

Finally, there is social knowledge, consisting of conventions worked out by people—for example, names or written labels for things, or the conventional algorithms for mathematical processes. This may be like Peirce's thirds, or logical concepts—how we know our world. But if these are imposed on learners before they have constructed the necessary logico-mathematical knowledge for themselves, all they can get from experience is physical knowledge, without true understanding.

Well, my "beginner's" interpretation is probably not quite accurate, but it adds a lot to what I'm messing around with. I had always considered mathematics to be a fixed body of knowledge. Since I've been exploring constructivism, I've been trying to figure out what it means in terms of my own understanding of mathematics and that of my students. I'm also trying to sort out how this fits with the transmission vs. transaction argument in the field of language, the idea that meaning is not inherent in the text but is only derived through the readers' construction of understanding (I think it fits perfectly). I have a lot to consider as I try to understand all this more deeply and place it within my own experience.

Now to Mayra: I liked your suggestion about listing all my hypotheses on one sheet, and I did so. I also did a similar listing with all my observations and interpretations. I hope it will help me better see the larger picture.

Today she read several pages of the Boxcar Children book. I found that writing down *what* she did was the easy part; interpreting it was hard. I really wasn't sure how to code some of the miscues. I'm not very confident about it and would appreciate some feedback.

And then, assuming I've made a reasonable analysis and come up with reasonably accurate percentages, where do I go from there? For example, it seems she is using grapho-phonemic cues consistently to try to "get the words," with many repetitions to confirm and correct. She's using semantic and syntactic cues in only about half her miscues, yet her retelling was excellent—complete, with all major concepts and specific information included. This is also very different from her reading last week when we started the story. So what do I make of all that? And what do I do with it? I need to begin examining the details more closely and try to figure out how it all fits. Well, I will hit the books and journals this week and see what I can find out.

October 10   In our time together this week, Mayra read the next section of the Boxcar Children book. The same pattern occurred as in last week's reading—many repetitions to confirm and some to correct, and again, an excellent and complete retelling. Most of her uncorrected miscues (there weren't too many) didn't affect the meaning, with one exception. The story segment contained a dialogue between two boys who were arguing over the outcome of a race their dogs had run the year before. Mike said his dog had beaten Benny's dog, and Benny said it was the other way around. Mayra consistently read the word *beat* as "bit" (a real word substitution, not a matter of dialect). To me, the miscue was logical and did make sense in a discussion about two dogs, but it tied in well with our following discussion of one of her recurring concerns about her reading.

She said this reading segment was easy because she "knew some of the words," and hard because "I forgot how to pronounce some of the words." She seems to talk a lot about pronouncing the words, so I asked her if you always have to know how to pronounce a word to understand its meaning. We looked at a few words where the pronunciation didn't matter, such as names. Then we looked at *beat* and *bit*, where it really did change the meaning. She concluded that you don't always have to know how to pronounce the words, but that there are times when you do. She also said that it helps to know the meanings of the words and that she looks in the dictionary when she doesn't know.

So what have I learned today? And where am I? I'm not sure. I'm still lost about her repetitions. I've been searching the references I have but haven't found much to go on. And I don't even know if it's something I should be dwelling on. I'm just not sure where to go from here. I keep going back to my feelings when I had her as a first and second grader: that all she needs are continued wide reading experiences to build her vocabulary and familiarity with written English. But that sounds so simplistic. There must be more and I'm just not seeing it. For now, I hate to say it, but I think I'm stuck.

October 16

A quick comment on semiotics á la Peirce versus constructivism via Piaget/Kamii (and then maybe we can get together to really look at this in depth sometime?). Peirce is not focusing on *types* of knowledge (á la Kamii) but rather is taking a phenomenological approach. He is not saying that firsts, seconds, and thirds are types of knowledge, but rather that these *are* the three categories of everything that is. His firsts are pre-perception and so are more like what Kamii says about a physical (sensory) knowledge. The understanding that is created is what Peirce would call a third and Kamii is calling logico-mathematical knowledge. Kamii seems to be making the naming part a third type of knowledge. Peirce would argue that labels are simply social conventions for the rule or concept to be understood. They function as signs but are not different from the rule or understanding with which they are associated (sort of).

I think it is easier (for me) to go from your reading example to Peirce/semiotics. Rosenblatt argues that the poem or meaning is created in transaction between the reader and the text. This seems to be Kamii's logico-mathematical knowledge and would be Peirce's thirdness.

A critical difference (about Peirce, from other philosophers), is that he argued that this thing we call knowledge is neither mind-dependent or mind-independent (a long-standing debate in philosophy). Kamii seems to believe in mind-independent, that things exist outside one's knowing. Instead, Peirce argued that all knowing is in relationship. This is a hard thing to get one's mind around at first, but I am thinking of doing a doctoral seminar on Peircean semiotics. Perhaps you might be interested in sitting in on it?

Back to Mayra: I've glanced at your coded transcript (see Figure 4) and miscue sheets and taken a look at the percentages you show in the three columns. It does seem that Mayra uses grapho-phonemics consistently. Yes, I can see that just glancing down your sheet. So she is trying phonics but it does not work very well and she seems to be privileging that rather than meaning. Not good.

You also say she is using semantics and syntactics about half the time. Not good. That means that half the time she backgrounds the meaning and privileges something else—grapho-phonemic info, it appears. As to the fact that she got a lot of meaning—that makes perfect sense to me (sorry, I've been at it a long time). She read 400 words and only made 30 miscues. That means she got more than 90% of the words. That's more than enough to carry the meaning.

Figure 4.
Excerpt of author's transcript of Mayra's reading, with miscues indicated.

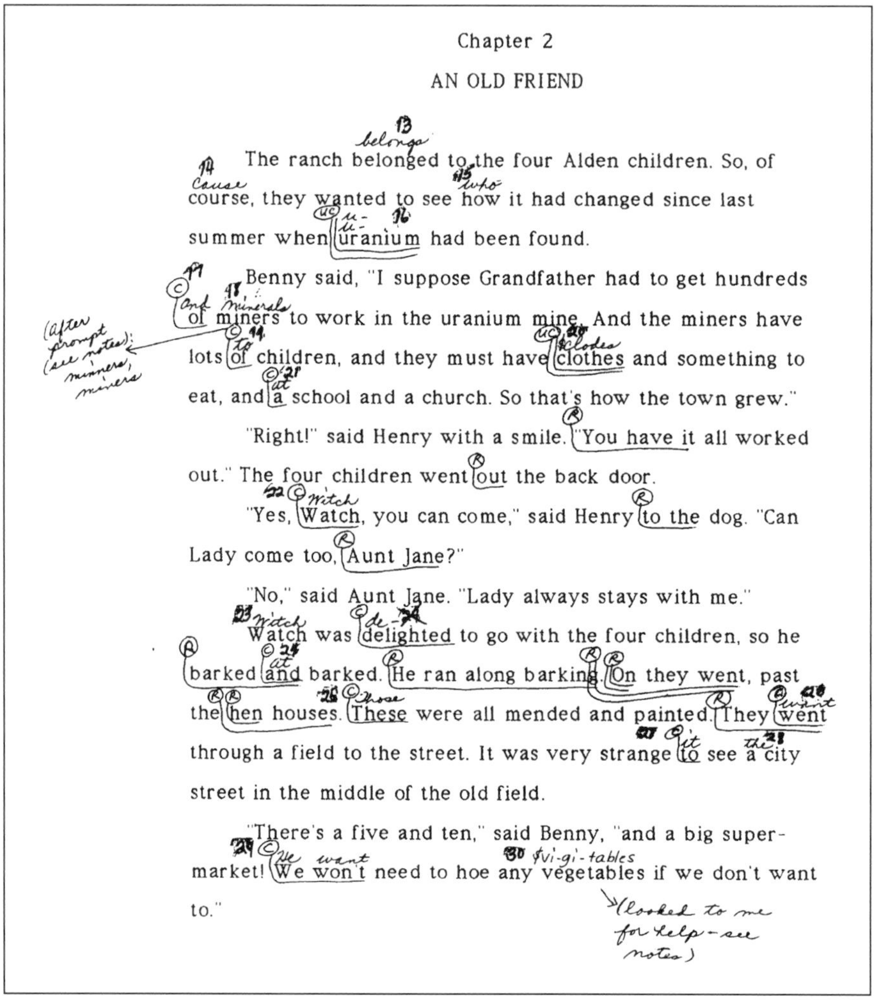

Chapter 2

AN OLD FRIEND

The ranch belonged to the four Alden children. So, of course, they wanted to see how it had changed since last summer when uranium had been found.

Benny said, "I suppose Grandfather had to get hundreds of miners to work in the uranium mine. And the miners have lots of children, and they must have clothes and something to eat, and a school and a church. So that's how the town grew."

"Right!" said Henry with a smile. "You have it all worked out." The four children went out the back door.

"Yes, Watch, you can come," said Henry to the dog. "Can Lady come too, Aunt Jane?"

"No," said Aunt Jane. "Lady always stays with me."

Watch was delighted to go with the four children, so he barked and barked. He ran along barking. On they went, past the hen houses. These were all mended and painted. They went through a field to the street. It was very strange to see a city street in the middle of the old field.

"There's a five and ten," said Benny, "and a big supermarket! We won't need to hoe any vegetables if we don't want to."

OK, let's see what she did when she corrected (Mayra/text):

ho/oh
it's/it is/is it
you been/you've seen
and/said
went/want
and/of
to/of
at/a
de/delighted
at/and
those/these
want/went
to/it
he want/ we won't

Looks to me as if her first guess is based on grapho-phonemic information and then she uses semantics and syntax to self-correct.
      Now let's see what she doesn't self-correct (Mayra/text):

was/has (little meaning change)
may/my (This was a weird sentence for her—for most kids, I think. I
      don't know anyone who even says, "Oh, my." Maybe she doesn't
      either. There certainly was not enough meaning for her to self-
      correct. After all, if a person can say "Oh, my", s/he could just as
      well have said, "Oh, may"!)
and/to (very little meaning change)
ser/serless/selves (unfamiliar word?)
belongs/belonged (very little meaning change)
cause/course   ???
who/how (common substitution when focus is not on meaning)
u/uranium (unfamiliar word?)
minerals/miners   ???
clodes/clothes (not in her sight vocab?)
witch/watch (but she gets it later)
the/a (no meaning change)
vi-gi-tables/vegetables

So these also look like she privileges grapho-phonemic information
and that, overall, leaving these words uncorrected in this passage did
not significantly affect the meaning of the passage. I am concerned,
however, because she does seem to privilege grapho-phonemic information. It seems to be her first line of attack when she doesn't know a
word.
      I also noticed all the repetitions. Do you think she is privileging
trying to get all the words right? Ah, I see you wondered that too. You
also wondered if the repetitions instead serve the meaning. That could
be too.

Something, though, is not quite right. Some of these are words that most fourth graders would have encountered in their reading and so would know as sight words. I wonder about how much she reads.

You end by saying that you go back to your feelings about her needing wide reading. That's my feeling too. That's why I was wondering about how much she reads. I am also wondering why she repeats so often. And I think it's an important puzzle to solve. I am concerned that her first guess is so tied to grapho-phonemics instead of meaning. Seems like she isn't predicting but word calling? Ah—and then, word in hand, goes back for meaning?

I too see this as challenging—and critical. It's partly why I get so frustrated when people try to sell teachers quick fixes. Teachers soon see that quick does not work and meanwhile, children lose out. I see no substitute for the hard work of understanding a child.

I feel like an announcer—guess I'll need to "stay tuned." I look forward to finding out what you find out. I enjoy taking this journey with you.

Mayra stands to gain a lot.

October 20   Thanks for the semiotics/constructivism information. It helped clarify a few things for me. I look forward to learning more, maybe next year?

You said, "Mayra stands to gain a lot." I wish I had your confidence! At this point, I feel I'm learning but I don't feel I am helping *her* at all. I feel you are offering me a lot of clues, but I guess I'm not making the connections yet. I feel I'm going around in circles and not seeing what is really important, or if I do sense that something is important, I don't know what to do with it. It makes me want to dig in deeper—but it is definitely frustrating!

I found your clustering of Mayra's miscues into two groups (corrected and uncorrected) to be helpful, in the same way the clustering of hypotheses helped. Thanks for that tip.

As for the amount of reading she does on her own, you are right—it's not much. I am trying to follow her lead in choosing books, which means concentrating mostly on the nonfiction she relishes so much. We agreed that I'd continue reading the Boxcar Children to her, and she will choose for her reading books on topics she wants to learn about. I hope I can help her find books she can read more successfully.

She wanted to learn about spiders. We found several books on the topic but the texts were quite difficult and rather technical. I had to paraphrase most of them for her. But even so, her questions weren't answered, so she decided to write them down and send them to an entomologist at a local museum I thought might help her.

We also started a book, *The Spooky Halloween Party* (Prager, 1981), designated as "easy to read." I wanted to see if she would still make all those repetitions with an easier text. She read a 175-word portion and made nine miscues, only one of which was not semantically or syntactically appropriate. Three of the nine miscues were repetitions to confirm and one was to correct. So she seems to repeat much less with an easier text (at least with this one). What does this mean? I'm not sure.

Anyway, I will make another stab at trying to understand what's going on—more reading and hard thinking. I know the pieces must be there—if only I could see them!

October 27   We shared the reading of some new books about spiders and we both learned a lot. Then we returned to *The Spooky Halloween Party*. Unlike last week, she made many repetitions, just as she was doing with the harder texts. I still don't know why she does this. She didn't seem to be struggling to read it, but I did feel the text wasn't that easy to get through. Maybe that's because it was written with a highly controlled vocabulary, so the language structure may not have been too helpful. I think I'll have to try better quality literature next time, something that flows more naturally and is more supportive of the reader.

But I did notice a couple of places where we could talk about predicting and/or putting in a word that makes sense as a desirable strategy. I reminded her of a game we used to play in her first- and second-grade years. We called it Silly Sentences. I'd say a sentence, leave out a word, and the kids would have to think of a word that made sense and started with a designated letter (the "silly" part referred to some of the ridiculous suggestions I'd offer). I had told the kids then that this strategy could help them when they were reading. We tried a few samples and Mayra realized it was kind of similar to what we were talking about in today's reading.

Then things began to click for me. Everything you've been saying—about setting the kids up for success, teaching for strategies, getting them to reflect on their strategies, etc.—is what I believe and try to do with my whole class. (In fact, it's exactly what I've been learning to do with math!) Why had I wondered if I was supposed to be doing something different when I worked with one child? For the first time, I really knew where I wanted to go next.

I told Mayra that I'd be having her read books that were even easier for her than *The Spooky Halloween Party*. I explained that I'd be looking for things she was doing that were helping her to read those books successfully, and we'd talk about them and see if they were things that could help her when she read harder books.

We did exactly that, with three very easy books, all by Cowley. I asked her how she had figured out some of the words she'd self-corrected, and she said she "knew it would make sense." We talked specifically about prediction as a useful strategy and why it was useful. I continued to have her explain her thinking as we went along. We related what she did to our Silly Sentences game and to what she did with subsequent books.

At one point, she looked back in the text to confirm something she was reading. When we talked about that, I shared with her the view of reading as a writing-like process: We don't have to read in one draft; returning to the text to gain greater understanding can be compared to revision in writing and is a desirable thing to do.

I asked her to try the two strategies she had demonstrated as she tackles her classroom reading next week, and to let me know if and how they helped her. She said she would.

I don't know if we're on to something or not, but we both felt good about the session. At least I felt I had a chance of starting to be helpful to her!

November 1   Let's see: When reading *The Spooky Halloween Party* she made 41 miscues out of 782 words, 19 of which she did not correct. (See Figure 5.) One of those she got correctly later in the story ("map"/*mop*). One may be dialect ("hang"/*hung*). She did this twice. Two may not have been in her oral vocabulary *(pirate, hissed)*. What does that leave?

who/how
dump/dumb
ha/oh
clothes, cloth? /clothes (relied on g-p and it got in her way?)
a/the (miscues five times on this)
eleven/elevator
c-/course
wouldn't/won't
opening/open
the/a (miscues once on this)
trouble/terrible
I/and
I am/I'm
sounded/sounds

I am not going to worry about "ha"/*oh* or about "I am"/*I'm* or "wouldn't"/*won't* or "a"/*the* or "the"/*a* because semantically they are fine. "Who"/*how* get frequently switched when the focus is either not on meaning or is on bigger meaning. "Eleven"/*elevator* we can't say much about because you say you ended up inadvertently giving it to her.

Reading Miscue Inventory Coding Sheet
© Carolyn L. Burke and Yetta M. Goodman 1972
Revised by Diane Stephens 1993

Reader: Mayra   Teacher: Diane Parker   Date: 10/24

Miscue Number	Reader	Corrected	Text	Semantically Acceptable			Grapho-Phonemically Acceptable			Syntactically Acceptable		
				Y	P	N	Y	P	N	Y	P	N
1	lead	√	lend		√			√			√	
2	map		mop			√		√				√
3	hang		hung	√				√			√	
4	who		how		√			√			√	
5	dump		dumb			√		√				√
6	she	√	this		√				√		√	
7	ne–	√	invited			√			√			√
8	parate		pirate			√	√					√
9	ha		oh	√					√		√	
10	hang		hung	√				√			√	
11	clothes—cloth?		clothes	√			√				√	
12	A		the	√					√		√	
13	Nicky	√	Nicky's		√			√			√	
14	eleven		elevator			√		√				√
15	clown	√	crown			√		√			√	
16	bear	√	pair		√			√			√	
17	cous–	√	cousin			√			√			√
18	s–	√	Suzanne			√			√			√
19	c–		course			√			√			√
20	wouldn't		won't	√				√		√		
21	to	√	at		√				√		√	
22	opening		open	√				√		√		
23	the		a	√					√	√		
24	gob–	√	goblin			√	√					√
25	a		the	√					√	√		
26	a		the	√					√	√		
27	a		the	√					√	√		
28	hiss-ed		hissed			√	√					√
29	trouble		terrible		√		√					√
30	cost	√	cast			√	√					√
31	pi–		pirates			√		√				√
32	I		and	√				√		√		
33	am		I'm	√				√		√		
34	a		the	√				√		√		
35	go–	√	goblin			√	√					√
36	sounded		sounds	√			√			√		
37	fall	√	fool			√	√				√	
38	hearded	√	headed			√	√					√
39	door–	√	doorbells			√	√					√
40	torn	√	turn			√	√					√
41	far–	√	faraway	√			√				√	
			Column Total	15	8	18	1	24	16	12	12	17
			Percentage	36	20	44	2	59	39	29	29	42

Figure 5. Miscue inventory sheet of another of Mayra's readings.

So do I end up worried? Not in terms of these books. But in terms of strategies, yes. She seems to make her first guess based on grapho-phonemic information. She doesn't seem to be using semantics to predict. As to why she keeps repeating? I don't know. It may serve as confirmation, or she may lack confidence (which could be the same thing).

I then went to your folder to look at her records so that I could think more about this. What I saw was that this strategy pattern seems to be consistent.

I think you are right that more predictable text may help her and I agree that within this level of difficulty, she would be able to learn (revalue) strategies such as making predictions. It seems that supporting and valuing strategies would help her with meaning making when she deals with text that has more unfamiliar words and so is more difficult for her. I would also try to pick materials in which she will encounter some unfamiliar words so that her vocabulary can be growing at the same time. Of course, it may be that almost all books afford this opportunity for her. I look forward to seeing where this goes next. I feel as if we are really getting somewhere. Hang in there. I think we almost have this solved!

November 3

This is all starting to come together for me. Here are my "pretty sures" and tentative curricular decisions, based on our conversations and on what hypotheses I've tested and confirmed so far:

When Mayra comes to a word she doesn't know, she seems to privilege grapho-phonemic information and word calling, rather than meaning making. When she knows most of the words in a book, this is hard to see, but it shows up in books which contain a number of words with which she is not familiar. In those books, she ends up repeating a lot, possibly to try to get the meaning, but the strategy she foregrounds, which is using grapho-phonemic information, means that repetition happens a lot.

In order to be more successful as a reader, Mayra needs a more balanced use of cueing systems and to put meaning in the foreground, using it to predict, and to use grapho-phonemic information to confirm.

I think what I have to do is continue helping her find books that will enable her to pursue her interests and that she can read successfully, to help her become aware of and build on the strategies she is using to read those books, and to help her develop new strategies. And I guess my other responsibility is to keep studying so I can be more informed and able to help her better.

November 10   The hypotheses you've tested out and the curricular decisions you've made are terribly important. It's important these strategies become part of her. Your work with her can change her future.

Also, I continue to worry about what she doesn't read at home. Do you have ideas to increase her out-of-school reading?

November 17   Thanks for the support about my hypotheses and curricular decisions. Here's hoping!

I, too, am concerned about Mayra's out-of-school reading. Because she lives in rather crowded conditions with a large extended family (including several babies and toddlers), it's difficult for her to find a quiet, uninterrupted time and space for reading. Maybe we can make some trips to the library together or figure out some other possibilities.

We worked today on the draft of her letter asking for information about spiders. She said she needed to correct some spelling errors, so I asked her to proofread it and circle the words she thought might be misspelled.

She found all her misspellings and also circled some words that were not misspelled. As we worked through each one, I tried the technique you told us about—having her think what letters might be in the word, what letters she was sure of, etc. It worked really well.

As she corrected her misspellings successfully, I asked her how she knew what letters to use. She said she remembered seeing the words in various books. Afterwards, I pointed out to her that in her 113-word letter, she had only nine misspelled words. She was very pleasantly surprised!

We then proofread for grammar. There weren't too many corrections needed, just a few changes from singular to plural. She realized the need for most of them herself as she read the letter aloud to me. Later, when she was copying her letter over, she found and changed one plural form to singular—we had both overlooked it earlier.

I asked her how things are going in her regular class. She said, "I'm knowing how to spell more words because I'm remembering them from reading." I told her that as she reads more, this will continue to happen. It was good to have the opportunity to talk about this reading–spelling connection, especially since she was making the connection for herself.

We finished the session by reading a couple of books she chose and working some more on strategies.

November 22   We read another book about spiders today. We both found the portion she read quite interesting. She read well and I felt the supporting factors, such as her interest in the subject and our background reading over the past few weeks, had a lot to do with her success. I was pleased to see that her percentage of semantically and syntactically acceptable (or partially acceptable) miscues was much greater than in earlier readings, and it seemed there was more of a balance across types of miscues (see Figures 6 and 7). I thought that the topic, text, support, and conditions seemed to play a big part in her being able to read effectively. I'm feeling that a lot more of the same would be good for her.

As for the nature of her miscues, I noticed that a lot of them (both corrected and uncorrected) simply involved her leaving the *-s* off the plural forms of words. I'm wondering about the reason. Could it be dialect? Not noticing word endings? Or what? And is it worth mentioning to her, or might that make her even more anxious to get every word "right"?

Figure 6.
Excerpt of author's transcript of Mayra's reading about spiders, with miscues indicated. Also see the corresponding miscue inventory sheet in Figure 7.

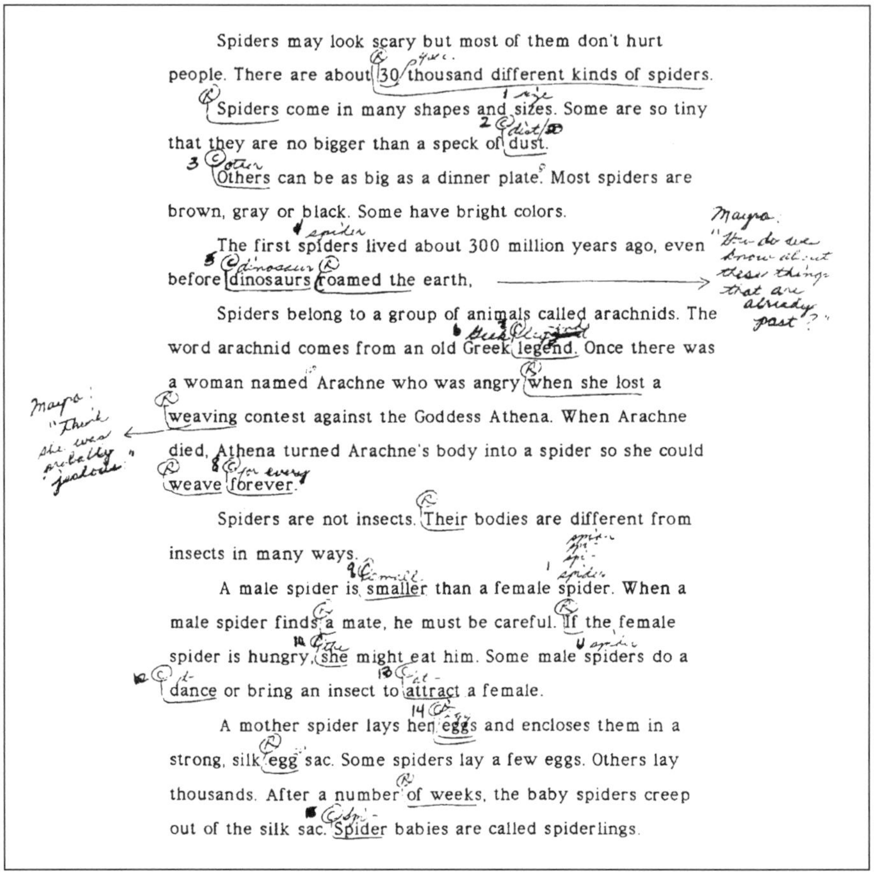

Spiders may look scary but most of them don't hurt people. There are about 30 thousand different kinds of spiders.

Spiders come in many shapes and sizes. Some are so tiny that they are no bigger than a speck of dust. Others can be as big as a dinner plate. Most spiders are brown, gray or black. Some have bright colors.

The first spiders lived about 300 million years ago, even before dinosaurs roamed the earth.

Spiders belong to a group of animals called arachnids. The word arachnid comes from an old Greek legend. Once there was a woman named Arachne who was angry when she lost a weaving contest against the Goddess Athena. When Arachne died, Athena turned Arachne's body into a spider so she could weave forever.

Spiders are not insects. Their bodies are different from insects in many ways.

A male spider is smaller than a female spider. When a male spider finds a mate, he must be careful. If the female spider is hungry, she might eat him. Some male spiders do a dance or bring an insect to attract a female.

A mother spider lays her eggs and encloses them in a strong, silk egg sac. Some spiders lay a few eggs. Others lay thousands. After a number of weeks, the baby spiders creep out of the silk sac. Spider babies are called spiderlings.

Reading Miscue Inventory Coding Sheet
© Carolyn L. Burke and Yetta M. Goodman 1972
Revised by Diane Stephens 1993

Reader: Mayra   Teacher: Diane Parker   Date: 11/14

Miscue Number	Reader	Corrected	Text	Semantically Acceptable			Grapho-Phonemically Acceptable			Syntactically Acceptable		
				Y	P	N	Y	P	N	Y	P	N
1	size		sizes	√			√				√	
2	dist	√	dust			√		√			√	
3	other	√	others		√		√				√	
4	spider		spiders	√			√			√		
5	dinosaur	√	dinosaurs	√				√			√	
6	Geek		Greek			√		√				√
7	leg-end	√	legend			√	√					√
8	for every	√	forever		√			√			√	
9	small	√	smaller	√				√		√		
10	the	√	she	√				√		√		
11	spider		spiders	√			√				√	
12	d–	√	dance			√			√			√
13	at–	√	attract			√			√			√
14	egg	√	eggs	√			√			√		
15	spi–	√	spider			√		√				√
16	a		the	√					√	√		
17	place		places	√			√			√		
18	streamer	√	streamers	√			√				√	
19	flies		lifts	√					√	√		
20	home		homes	√			√			√		
		Column Total		12	2	6	9	7	4	8	7	5
		Percentage		60	10	30	45	35	20	40	35	25

Figure 7. The miscue inventory sheet that corresponds with the text Mayra read, shown in Figure 6.

We talked for a while about her reading at home and at school. She has been reading to her younger sisters a little, which is good. And her mom, Aida, is reading to all of them as part of a community college course she is taking to improve her own reading and writing. Aida has been borrowing books from me and I've been helping her with some of her projects. Her current project requires her to demonstrate a creative way to present a story to young children. She decided to have her classmates act out *The Three Little Pigs* (Rounds, 1992), and she asked me for help with her preparations. We read and discussed the book together so she could become familiar with the story. It was quite an experience for me to read this with an adult who didn't grow up with this story! She just loved the part when the wolf went down the chimney. She laughed just like the kids do!

We brainstormed some possibilities for dramatizing the story. She had some good, creative ideas. I suggested she have her daughters help her, and she did. She called me that evening and said they were all busy drawing and cutting out props, and that the girls were going to go to class with her and help her with the acting! I thought that sounded great. Unfortunately, the class was canceled on the day they were scheduled to do their presentation, and she doesn't know if or when it will be rescheduled. I hope they get to do it. I think it would be neat for the girls to see where their mom goes to school and to share in an experience there with her.

November 29

Mayra's miscues on the plural forms of words could be dialect. It's not as likely that she's not noticing word endings. I would say it's not worth calling to her attention—I agree that it might make her even more anxious about getting words "right." Besides, it's not a *reading* problem.

Great that they're doing more reading at home. I hope they will be able to do their presentation in Aida's class.

December 6

[Excerpts from author's summary paper.] When this semester began, I felt I knew Mayra very well as a person and as a mathematics learner. I did not think I had ever looked as closely at her reading and I wondered if I would come to know her differently by focusing on her as a reader.

Was I surprised by what I found out? Not really, now that I look back. Did it help me to think through some of the questions I've had about her reading? Yes, it did.

These are some of the strengths I had listed as I worked with Mayra in mathematics:

1. She has a wonderful desire to learn, to know.

2. She drives herself to learn. She knows what she needs or wants to work on and makes a deliberate attempt to do it.

3. She will ask and ask until she is satisfied that she understands. She strives constantly to make sense of mathematics for herself.

4. She is willing to work hard and to put in as much time as it takes to accomplish her goals. She is willing to persevere in mathematical tasks.

5. She uses a problem-solving approach to investigate and understand mathematical content.

6. She develops and applies her own strategies to solve problems. She often uses and relates pictures and diagrams to mathematical ideas.

7. She is able to explain what she is doing and why as she solves problems.

8. She notices and explains connections.

9. She shows flexibility in exploring mathematical ideas.

10. She shows interest, curiosity, and inventiveness in doing mathematics. She is a problem poser.

11. She approaches mathematical tasks with confidence.

After reviewing Mayra's general strengths, I took a look in more detail at some of the mathematical ideas and tasks we had worked on and at my notes and observations related to those tasks. Here is one example:

> [When she was in the third grade, Mayra had asked me to help her with her multiplication tables; she wanted to memorize them for quick recall and felt she had not yet mastered this task.]
> As we organized and examined the multiplication chart together, she was surprised to see she already knew more facts than she had thought. . . . Organizing it all and taking a look at it, as we did, helped her to see the larger picture and realize the relationships. . . . It made me realize once again the importance of the talking and the types of questions that can help to focus the talking. As we studied and searched for patterns together, she began to see some sense in the chart and it stopped seeming like an overwhelming task to learn it.

I also looked at some other general notes from our work in mathematics. One thing I noticed was a pattern which had developed as she moved to the higher grades: she seemed to worry more and more about report card and test grades, teacher disapproval, and being "correct."

As I reflected on my notes, I found myself making mental comparisons with what we've been doing in reading and saying, "Aha!"

Next, I considered the mathematics list, point by point, in terms of my notes and HT sheets related to Mayra's reading, and this is where "Aha!" became "AHA!!" Here are my comparisons, sketched briefly:

1. Her desire to learn, to know: I see it clearly and constantly, in her questions and desire to explore many topics.

2. Her drive to learn: I see this also, both in her presence in this class and her constant search for knowledge.

3. Her striving to make sense of things: I see this in our talking all the time.

4. Her willingness to work hard: No doubt here. As for her willingness to persevere: I see it, but she needs much more support than with math because of her view of herself as a poor reader.

5. Her use of a problem-solving approach to investigate and under-stand math: Hmm, is she doing this with reading? It is such a great strength of hers in math. What can I do to help her utilize it more fully as a reader?

6. Her development and application of problem-solving strategies: I see a parallel with reading strategies (for example, estimating or number sense in math seems kind of like predicting in reading). She also uses pictures and diagrams as a reader in the same way she uses them as a mathematics learner, and I think that's good.

7. Her ability to explain what she's doing and why: I have to keep helping her use this strength as we work on reading strategies.

8. Her noticing of connections: I see it in her reading all the time.

9. Her flexibility in exploring ideas: Will building her repertoire of strategies help her with this? I hope so.

10. Her interest and problem posing in math: I think it's there in her reading, but I need to help her become more aware of it.

11. Her confidence in approaching math: *Uh-oh,* this may be the biggest need of all with her reading!

Then I reviewed the first four goals for mathematics learners in the NCTM *Curriculum and Evaluation Standards* document (1989).

These are broad (not content-specific) standards that I believe can serve to guide all learning, not just mathematics. They are:

Mathematics as problem solving.

Mathematics as connections.

Mathematics as reasoning.

Mathematics as communication.

I then replaced *mathematics* with *reading*:

Reading as problem solving.

Reading as connections.

Reading as reasoning.

Reading as communication.

Does it fit? I think it fits perfectly. Good readers most certainly demonstrate all the above qualities. Mayra demonstrates them in mathematics; so how can I help her to do the same with reading, because they must all be a part of her already?

To find out, I went back to some of my notes and readings on constructivism, which have guided me as I've worked with her in math. I have felt all along that it would be possible to use what I know about Mayra as a mathematics learner to help her as a reader. It was finally time to put my theory to the test.

According to Kamii (1990), in a constructivist approach to mathematics learning, there are three kinds of knowledge: physical, or empirical, knowledge; logico-mathematical knowledge, consisting of self-created relationships constructed from the inside; and social knowledge, or the conventions worked out by people. Learners must construct their own knowledge in order to truly understand social knowledge in more than a surface way. In her article, Kamii argues that this theory has powerful implications for teaching. Here are three she mentions:

1. We have to focus on children's thinking rather than on their writing correct answers. We have to help them use the knowledge they have to figure out the unknown. I have realized that this is what I need to do with Mayra: to help her build on the strengths and strategies she is using; to concentrate more on *what and how she is thinking* as she reads. I see it as taking a problem-solving approach to reading. Mayra expects math to make sense, and she uses good strategies to make sense of it for herself. I need to help her see that reading should make sense also and to help her develop and internalize strategies to make sense of what she reads in the same way.

2. We have to encourage discussion and debate so children will have the opportunity to examine their own thinking and to construct a

higher level of thinking. This means that learners must feel safe to express their own opinions honestly. I have realized that Mayra lacks confidence in herself as a reader, and therefore I must help by making reading as safe as math is for her. I need to create reading situations that will interest her and in which she can be successful. I need to encourage her with the types of open-ended questions I use in mathematics discussions, to help her articulate her thinking and keep the focus on meaning. I also need to continue to help her realize, organize, and *name* (constructivism/semiotics!) what she knows and to see the "bigger picture." Just as with the multiplication example earlier, she was pleasantly surprised to realize she was able to predict words successfully in several stories and to spell most of the words correctly in her letter. I think this can be an important factor in her confidence-building.

    3. We should use situations in daily living to help children construct knowledge out of real-life problems. I see a parallel here with Mayra's strong interest in nonfiction and her insatiable desire to learn about the world around her. I need to continue to help her find books and other appropriate resources to explore the things she cares deeply about. Through researching her own real questions, she will, I hope, want to read more. Through discussion and context-based problem solving, she will, I hope, become a proficient reader.

    So, do I know Mayra differently now? Yes and no, I guess. It might be more accurate to say that I know her better now. Generally, her personality and character traits seem consistent across subject areas, as I had expected them to be. More specifically, I think *the differences that have emerged lie in the way she approaches reading as compared with the way she approaches math.* I hope I can help her to revalue both her concept of reading and her view of herself as a reader, ideally to bring them into alignment with her concept of math and her view of herself as a mathematics learner. I think this is crucial to her development as a reader. It's going to be difficult, but I believe it's possible. I know it's in her—I just hope it's in me, too!

Epilogue

Mayra continued to try using the strategies we worked on during the rest of her fourth-grade year, but it was a struggle. She felt she was not using them consistently or automatically. By the fifth grade, however, she told me that she was beginning to "remember" and use them in her reading. That year she was in a heterogeneously grouped class where a strategic approach to reading was valued and taught, and where quality literature was studied and enjoyed by the teacher and students together. In sixth grade, her reading classes were again grouped homogeneously, but Mayra was placed in the "top" reading group, where she was described by her teacher as one of the best readers in the class. Her sixth-grade standardized test scores in reading were all in the "above average" range. Mayra has just completed eighth grade and has been an honor roll student. Her current goal is to go to college and become a teacher.

References

Cowley, J. (1987a). *Little car.* Bothell, WA: The Wright Group.

Cowley, J. (1987b). *Ratty tatty.* Bothell, WA: The Wright Group.

Cowley, J. (1987c). *Red socks and yellow socks.* Bothell, WA: The Wright Group.

Kamii, C. (1990). Constructivism and beginning arithmetic (K–2). In *Teaching and learning mathematics in the 1990s.* Reston, VA: National Council of Teachers of Mathematics.

National Council of Teachers of Mathematics. (1989). *Curriculum and evaluation standards for school mathematics.* Reston, VA: National Council of Teachers of Mathematics.

Prager, A. (1981). *The spooky Halloween party.* New York: Pantheon.

Rounds, G. (1992). *The three little pigs and the big bad wolf.* New York: Holiday House.

Warner, G. C. (1988). *Mike's mystery.* Niles, IL: Albert Whitman and Co.

III Learning *from* One-on-One: HT in the Classroom

Introduction

8

Jennifer Story

Details the experiences of four teachers after they had a solid understanding of the HT process. Shows how HT can be used with an entire class and explains that the insights gained from using the HT process also often impact curriculum.

I learned HT when I was a full-time graduate student working as a tutor during a teaching sabbatical. What I learned was how to know one child as a reader well enough to make a difference in the life of that child as a reader. When I returned to the classroom full time, I began the year feeling confident that I could now help all my struggling readers. However, I quickly felt overwhelmed. I knew how to help a child one-on-one, and I knew how to plan for and work with groups of children. But how could I ever know enough—spread myself around enough—to know *every* child, to help *every* child? I had to merge the roles of tutor and classroom teacher. I had to find a way to really see and know every child in the class, in the large group, the trio, the dyad.

Eventually, I accomplished this by coming up with record-keeping systems that allow me to keep track of each and every child. Sometimes I keep a file folder for each child, and other years, I keep a three-ring binder tabbed for each individual. These two simple collection systems have their advantages: both make it easy to add other artifacts of kids' work, portfolio-style, such as telling samples of writing, reading interviews, or photocopies of math journal entries, and it is easy to use either method to add pages on which to record interpretations, hypotheses, and curricular decisions. The advantage of folders is that they allow several adults to share them to record observations at the same time. Folders are also easier to take to parent–counselor–teacher conferences. A binder, however, pushes the teaching team to talk about each child, from the first tab to the last. Oftentimes just mentioning the child's name will remind one of us of an observation, or even a lack of observations—as in the case of J.R.

Recently, I noticed that we had very few observations of J.R., yet he was one of the kids I had said early on that I wanted to know more about. Now I have to wonder about why J.R. is not attracting observations. Is he doing OK? Is he sliding past us? Why did I think he needed special attention in the first place? I think I'd better make an effort to scrutinize his work and take a closer look at him in action.

My most important consideration in choosing a method of record keeping is that it enables me to record observations as they occur. I often use sticky-notes or address labels; sticky-notes are particularly handy because they fit in my pocket and I can always find some lying around the classroom. When I'm noting an observation, I just write the date and name of the kid and a phrase to remind me of the observation, like "reluctant to put chair in group circle again!" When I consolidate notes I attach the sticky-note to the child's pages in either folder or binder, and if I need to, explicate the sometimes cryptic notes so that I won't lose the details of the observation.

Address labels (an idea Heidi Mills originated) are useful when I am organized enough to be using a clipboard. They have an advantage over sticky-notes in that it is easy to run on to the next label if my observation notes are more extensive, and also they stick handily into the child's consolidated notes without tape.

A third option for keeping observations is to use notebook paper, which is readily available but requires transcribing or cutting and pasting my notes.

In the past few years, e-mail has become one of my most important modes of record keeping and thinking. A small group of classroom teachers, student teachers, and university faculty have developed what we call the "fish bowl," so named because we are willing to expose our innermost thoughts and feelings about what is going on in our classrooms. It has become a forum that helps initiate preservice teachers as well as a first-semester probationary teacher as she finds her way in a new position. Our dialogue in this "fish bowl" helps us to understand our students and ourselves through the way of thinking that HT has caused us to "try on," adopt, and adapt. The vocabulary of HT has become a part of our conversation as we advise each other to step back and take another look, to trace out and explain more closely what might seem to one of us to be a leap in decision making.

What happens when you try on HT, I think, is that the record keeping and the way of thinking drive each other to evolve. I began— and recommend that you begin—by using HT with one child you are worried about, rather than with a whole class. Using the basic HT grid designed by Diane Stephens (see Figure 1 in Chapter 1) can help organize this complex process. Although our discussions in the "fish bowl" started from the same structure—the observation/interpretation/ hypothesis/curricular decisions cycle—it has evolved so that HT is integral to our seemingly intuitive hypotheses and curricular decisions.

In the last section of this book, three other teachers write about where the HT path has taken them. Like me, Sandie Kubota discovered that HT was a useful way to understand each and every child in our classrooms. She details how she used the HT process to learn about one child, Mei Ling. Two other teachers' one-on-one HT experiences led them to rethink their curriculum. Betty Ito began by comparing what she had learned about Ho'olai, a first grader, with how she was teaching reading and writing in her seventh- and eighth-grade classroom for children who were labeled "special education students." Paula Matsunaga compared her learning through HT with the types of curricular experiences she had been setting up for her first graders. For both of them, their experiences with HT one-on-one led to curricular transformations.

We hope readers are beginning to appreciate why we value HT: Not only does it help us understand particular children at particular points in time, but *as a way of thinking*, it is a generative process that transforms our lives and the lives of our students.

Mei Ling

Sandie Kubota
Central Oahu District, Hawaii

Shows HT in action in the classroom and celebrates author's success with using HT to help a child in her first/second-grade classroom.

Mei Ling is one of my twenty-five second-grade students. I have the privilege of working with my students for two years, starting off with them as first graders then moving up with them into the second grade—an arrangement we refer to as looping.

Mei Ling started first grade in our school two weeks later than the rest of her classmates. Our school year starts at the beginning of August, and Mei Ling, whose family had just moved into the community, had been attending a school that operated on the more traditional school calendar. By the time she entered our classroom, our community was becoming established; we had been gelling together into a cohesive group of individuals for two weeks. My job and the job of the children was to help Mei Ling become a member of that community, to help her to get to know the other children and our procedures as quickly as possible. Everyone else had had those ten days, and she was at a disadvantage. Nevertheless, the children accepted her quickly and we all made sure that she was included in everything we did. At the same time, I needed to get to know her as well as I already knew the others. I particularly looked forward to understanding how she used reading and writing in her learning process.

On Mei Ling's first day in the classroom, one of her tasks was to write in her writing journal. Everyone else had started their first day of first grade the same way. The assignment was to write about what is important to you and about what has been on your mind lately. As Mei Ling took out her crisp, black-and-white composition book and pencil, I sat next to her to be sure that she understood the assignment. I wanted to know how she used writing to make sense of her experiences and to see how she used writing as a tool to communicate her ideas. Mei Ling sat at her desk quietly, pausing with the pencil in her hand. I inferred from her hesitation that she was thinking about how to begin the given assignment. Soon she began to etch out the first letter of her first word.

After a few moments, I left her side to give her some "breathing space" and so she could feel trusted in her attempts. I walked around the classroom, conferring with other children, asking them to tell me what they were writing about by reading back to me the written text, commenting on their sharing, and asking questions if I did not understand something. With the students who seemed to be off to a good start, I checked to see if they had a direction they were taking in their writing. During all of these conversations, I purposely spoke loudly enough so to give Mei Ling a sense of what our conferences were like. I wanted her to feel comfortable, to know that I was not concerned about the mechanics of the writing—just the ideas, the reading and writing connections that people make in the process. I wanted her to know that mechanics would not be important until we published our writing.

Gradually I worked my way back to Mei Ling's desk and looked over her shoulder, trying not to be obvious. She had written one phrase, *TODAY MY MOM*. My experience with the HT way of thinking helped me realize that there was much to understand about what she had written. First, I noted that when asked to write about what was important to her, Mei Ling wrote about her mother. I asked her to read to me what she had written, because I wanted to understand her ideas about writing and how she used writing to help herself think. She was able to read the words she had written, but did not realize that it was not a complete thought. When I asked her to tell me more, she said that her mom was going to the store, taking her to Ice Palace, and then returning home. I asked Mei Ling if she would like to add what she just told me into her writing, and she said that she would. I wanted to probe some more but decided not to; I thought that because it was her first day, she needed to first feel a part of our group. I did not want to push her, to make her feel she had to open up if she was not ready to do so. I wanted to let her write when she felt comfortable doing so. I walked away and hoped that she would add what we talked about to her initial phrase. At the end of the day, I checked her writing journal again and saw that she had not written anything other than those first three words.

Mei Ling was a lot like several of my other first graders. She seemed to have some concepts of print, and from my observation, she was pretty much at the level of what would be expected of most first graders on the first day of school. Although she had written only this one phrase, I was not worried or concerned. I was happy that she could write as she did. Based on my observations from that first day, I brainstormed the following interpretations:

She may know how to spell some words conventionally.

She may think that words need to be spelled correctly whenever she writes.

She may be hesitant to write what she does not know how to spell.

She may not understand that writing is putting down one's thoughts.

She may not understand that it is OK to write what she is thinking.

She may think she was supposed to write what I wanted her to write.

She may be reluctant to take any risks on her first day in a new setting (or on any day?).

She may not have felt comfortable in the room; she may have felt like an outsider.

She may not feel confident in our classroom yet.

As the days passed, I kept a close eye on Mei Ling. In the HT process, interpretations don't always lead right away to hypotheses. Sometimes, I need more observations and interpretations before I can generate a hypothesis. I've learned it is best not to come to any quick fixes, for these hasty decisions do not give a child the benefit that comes from reflection on the observations. Both my student teacher and I began to compare Mei Ling's reading and writing to that of her peers. We noticed that her progress was relatively slow; she seemed to be especially struggling in her oral and written language.

One day Mei Ling tried to ask me if she could retrieve the plastic hanger holding the chart paper on which I had written the children's ideas regarding the story elements of *Lyle, Lyle, Crocodile* (Waber, 1965). That day the children were writing down their own retellings of the story and could refer to the chart to help recall the details we had discussed together. Mei Ling came up to me and asked, "Mrs. Kubota, can I use the, uh, uh?" I was not sure to what she was referring, so I asked her, "Tell me again, Mei Ling, what do you need?" She pointed toward the front of the room and answered, "The thing. You know, the thing." I was still baffled. She then added, "The thing to go in front?" Finally, through the process of elimination and through the context of the assignment, I was able to narrow down the items until we finally understood each other. "Oh, the chart paper!" I answered, with much relief. Mei Ling nodded in agreement and we both began to laugh about the situation. I wanted to make light of the situation, and I now knew Mei Ling well enough to know that in these situations, she would always give me her shy smile with a soft giggle following. I told her she could get the chart; she got it and put it in front of the chalkboard for everyone to use. Based on these and other observations, I brainstormed these interpretations:

English may not be Mei Ling's first language. (In addition to observations I'd made about Mei Ling, I'd noticed her parents had an accent.)

Mei Ling might not have known the expression "chart paper."

Mei Ling might have felt uncomfortable asking me a question.

Mei Ling might not have felt comfortable asking to change something in the room.

Mei Ling may not yet understand the rules of our community.

Mei Ling may not have had enough interactions outside of school with children her age to provide situations where she must apply and practice her oral language.

Mei Ling may not have as many words in her oral vocabulary as others her same age.

Looking across all my interpretations (for that day as well as for other days), I hypothesized that English was her second language. I decided to check her student record: Her mother was born in Malaysia and her father was from Singapore; however, English was listed as her primary language. I called her parents to verify the records, and they explained that they used English at home and that "no other language" was spoken. With this information, I decided to observe her more and to do so in as many situations as possible. Having found that English was the spoken language at home, I revisited my observations and interpretations and changed my hypothesis to "Mei Ling may have some difficulty processing oral language."

To test this hypothesis, I solicited the aid of a speech pathologist. With permission from Mei Ling's parents, the speech pathologist administered an informal language assessment. All indications from the assessment were that Mei Ling had no difficulties processing oral or written language. Having disproved my first two hypotheses, I decided to observe her some more and generate other interpretations and other hypotheses.

I began to notice that whenever our class discussed content-area ideas or concepts as a group, Mei Ling was often very quiet—so quiet that I could not determine how much she understood and was learning. She did not approach me privately either, to share with me something that she thought about. She was cordial and sought me out during my recess duty days, wanting to carry my fanny pack (emergency pack) and to be helpful in other ways. I desperately wanted to know what was going on in her head, but it was difficult because she said very little.

I continued to use the HT process, and by the time parent–teacher conference rolled around in October, I was pretty sure I understood what was going on: Mei Ling was not willing to risk saying much in large-group situations. My curricular decision was to tell her that I was certain she knew a lot of things and that if she would volunteer some of her thoughts in class, we could all see how much she knew. Around this same time, we were having large-group discussions in our "community circle." As part of this, we would take turns discussing topics related to our content study or other topics. We'd all

agreed to listen attentively, respect each other (no put-downs allowed), and that each person had the right to pass. After Mei Ling
and I talked, she began to participate wholeheartedly in these circles.
By the end of the school year, she even spoke up in other large-group
discussions. I celebrated every effort that she made. She was using
more words and explaining her thoughts. Her contributions to the
discussions began to be deeper as she made evident her thinking.

Learning about the Writer and Reader

At the same time I was using the HT process to try to understand Mei
Ling's oral language patterns, I was using it to learn about her as
writer and reader.

When writing, she often seemed to find it hard to get down her
thoughts. For example, one day I noticed that, after working for a
long time, she had written:

> I wat to the farimap wan I Pas my far pas I wat to my fat pas I wat to
> the lag sli.
> [I went to the fair when I pass my favorite place I went to my favorite
> place I went to the long slide.]

She seemed to understand sound–symbol relationships, but her
understandings were not consistently conventional. Her spelling skills
seemed to be at what Gentry and Gillet (1993) consider the pre-
communicative level. I made a number of other observations and
interpretations during this time, which led to hypotheses I tested
through further observations.

I soon became pretty sure that Mei Ling did not have much
experience with writing, so my curricular decision became to support
her by giving her more time to develop as a writer. This meant that I
needed to allow her the time to just work on writing, especially free
writing. Conferring with her individually more frequently also seemed
to help. When she read me what she had written, I asked questions
such as, "Does that make sense to you?" "If it doesn't, how could you
make it have the sense that you want?" By then, too, spelling was part
of our writers' workshop time. We worked on phonemic skills, using
words from the children's writing and using a strategy called "try-it-
out spelling," in which the children try to spell a word that they are
not sure of and then check it with their peers, the teacher, or the
dictionary.

Meanwhile, through the HT process, I came to understand that
Mei Ling was an emergent reader, one who did not use picture cues
to help with unfamiliar words but who did try to sound out some
letters in some of the unknown words she encountered. She seemed
to view reading as decoding, rather than as a process of making
meaning from print. Her ability to retell text that she read on her own
or that was read to her was often very limited. She could remember

specific details but could not remember the sequence of events. She often could not tell me what the text meant to her personally. Her responses frequently centered on her likes or dislikes about particular story elements from the text, ("I liked this story because I like dogs"). I realized that she did not have a variety of strategies for making sense of print and that she needed my support to acquire and use those strategies.

I also was pretty sure that Mei Ling needed more support than some of the other children. By October, many of her classmates were excelling in their reading and writing. They were using reading and writing to make sense of texts across content areas, but Mei Ling was still struggling. I also knew that when we went on to second grade, reading and writing would become even more involved, and I did not want to see Mei Ling fall behind.

In every classroom, there inevitably is a range of abilities in the students. Some children take to reading and writing like a fish takes to water, others need a little more time or support, and some need much, much more support and creative thinking on the part of the teacher. I hypothesized that Mei Ling fell into this third category. My curricular decision then was to think of ways I could provide the kind of support that she needed. I talked with her parents and provided them with some suggestions about how to help her with her reading at home. I asked them to continue reading aloud to her, to have her read those texts that she could handle on her own, and made suggestions for how they could respond to her as a reader. Based on my suggestion, Mei Ling's parents enrolled her in an after-school tutoring program at our school. The purpose of these twice-a-week sessions was to immerse her in as many literature and literacy activities as possible. I also began to work with her individually in class, sometimes in a small group of three children. I asked her to think aloud to me as we worked together so that I could try to get a glimpse of what was happening in her head. I tried to be sure that all the literacy activities in the classroom were personally meaningful for her.

A Journey of Learning

Mei Ling became a source of wonderment throughout the year. At the end of school, I stepped back and took a hard look at what Mei Ling could do. Where was she on this journey of learning? Her speaking skills had improved tremendously. Her ability to take risks had become and continued to be more and more evident each day. As a writer, she was aware of what a sentence looks like—that it has a noun and verb—and her ideas were now more focused. She added more details to her writing. In spelling, she went from Gentry and Gillet's (1993) pre-communicative level to the phonetic level. Her words were beginning to look more conventional. As a reader, she had made considerable progress. She used several strategies to help herself make meaning from print. She used picture cues, read ahead, reread, made predictions. She more consistently used her knowledge of phonics. And although I use the results of the Stanford Achievement Test as additional data, I was pleased to see that her total reading score fell in the "average" stanine 4 range. Her mother was very happy to see her scores, too. What progress she made!

Using the HT process with Mei Ling helped me make sense of who she was as a person and as a learner. Judith Newman (personal communications, 1997) said that you can not make a child want to learn, the wanting comes from the child. I could see this coming into play for Mei Ling. She arrived in my classroom wanting to learn. I saw her as needing support in order to reach her goals. The HT process helped me help her do this.

Mei Ling taught me over and over again that making hasty conclusions about behaviors does not benefit the learner. Seeking out more evidence via observations, inferring from the evidence (interpretations), looking for patterns and generating hypotheses, testing the hypotheses, and then making more observations and interpretations and hypotheses is crucial. Using this process enables teachers to provide the understanding and support that learners need. In going through this process with Mei Ling, I was forced to constantly think about how I was creating the structure and environment of my classroom. I kept having to go back to Diane Stephens' words (personal communications, 1994): "What matters? What do you value in your teaching? How do you demonstrate your value in your teaching?" These are questions that I continuously ask myself because I am a learner, too. If I judge too quickly, I close the door to other possibilities. If I leave the door open, I am certain to catch the winds of those what-ifs.

Another important lesson Mei Ling taught me as we went through the HT process is that the things that occur in my classroom can not happen randomly. I value learning; therefore, I must structure my classroom so that I have a direction toward which we will head. This is what matters to me. Some children may need more time to get to the destination, and some will be ahead of the others. Then there are those who will find their own path. That is all right. What matters is that I have set up a structure that will help each child find her or his own way along this journey of learning.

The path I have taken from my first engagement with the HT process a half-decade ago never seems to end. My children—Mei Ling and all the others—and I walk this path together, side by side. I don't see myself leading the journey, but rather as a guide when someone seems to fall along the wayside or needs a boost. And then I think, what if I hadn't begun to take this path—what would my teaching look like? I can not help but think about the last verse in Robert Frost's poem, "The Road Not Taken":

> I shall be telling this with a sigh
> Somewhere ages and ages hence:
> Two roads diverged in a wood, and I—
> I took the one less traveled by,
> And that has made all the difference.

> (From Untermeyer's *Robert Frost, The Road Not Taken*)

References   Gentry, J. R., & Gillet, J. W. (1993). *Teaching kids to spell.* Portsmouth, NH: Heinemann.

Untermeyer, L. (Ed.). (1977). *Robert Frost, the road not taken: A selection of Robert Frost's poems.* New York: Henry Holt.

Waber, B. (1965). *Lyle, Lyle, crocodile.* New York: Houghton Mifflin.

Learning with Ho'olai

Bette Ito
Wahiawa Middle School, Hawaii

Describes how author changed the reading and writing curriculum in her special education seventh- and eighth-grade classes as a result of learning HT with a first grader.

After sixteen years as a secondary language arts teacher, I had the opportunity to work with a five-year-old child, Ho'olai, as part of a class I took on the HT process. When we first met, Ho'olai and I "talked story" about what she wanted to learn. Ho'olai said she "wanted to learn to read better," "to learn to write," and to make her handwriting "nice." When I asked her what she wanted to do in our sessions together, she said she wanted to read a lot. Ho'olai suggested I choose a story to read to her and she would choose a book to read to me.

That was OK with me: She was laying out an agenda for us, and I was happy to follow her lead. I wanted her to take me on her learning journey. I wanted her to show me what she already knew and what she wanted to learn. (I could take this risk because I wasn't supposed to be teaching her, I was supposed to be learning about her.) In the end, I realized that every time we met, I learned something from her about teaching.

What I learned from Ho'olai changed my ideas about how reading and writing are learned and how they should be taught. By watching Ho'olai read picture books, then predictable books, then books that still had pictures but had longer story lines, I saw that—on her own—she was able to make connections between what she was reading and written language. In every encounter she was learning language, learning about language, and learning through language (Halliday, 1973). I watched as she made the leap from not being able to associate letters to sounds, sounds to words, and words to phrases to all of a sudden being able to make those connections and know how to use context clues to figure out new words.

In the past, I'd equated reading with story grammar. I'd believed reading needed to be taught in sequential fragments. I taught students to understand a story by taking it apart element by element, worksheet by worksheet. Students had to be taught how to understand the parts before they could understand the whole story. In working with Ho'olai, I learned this wasn't true. I did not teach her story grammar, yet she was able to identify the main characters in the story and understand the theme, the setting, and how problems were solved. She figured these things out for herself. The names for these elements came up naturally in our conversations.

I also used to think that teaching reading was figuring out what the students' problems were and then teaching to the problems. I used to worry first about the technical stuff: Can he sound out all the words correctly? Does she say the correct sounds? Is phrasing correct? Is there fluency? To teach these skills, I used basals and teacher's manuals and skill-and-drill sheets and boring books. Now I am more holistic. I look at how much comprehension is going on and what connections are taking place. I deal with reading as a whole instead of as a fragmented process. Students choose their own books and stories. We talk about the meaning of the story, what sorts of personal experiences the students bring to the story, and what kinds of understanding they get out of it. Students bring their experiences into the classroom, make their own connections, and, as a result, understand more about themselves as well as about the story. I teach skills and strategies within this context.

I've also changed my ideas about teaching writing. I used to assign writing topics and provide detailed writing requirements. Now students write for themselves—to make sense of what they read, of their lives, of how everything connects together. I write with them. I share my drafts, my reflections, and my reactions to books I've read. I invite them to try different types of writing and to read different genres. I share a wide variety of books with them—some that I love, some that they may like, and some that I think they need. They and I keep a reading–writing log and a writing folder. We save all our work. We each choose which pieces we want to revise and publish. Each of us has a portfolio for our important best pieces, separate from our "working" folder. My students and I look at our folders, evaluate what we've done so far, and plan our learning journey together.

I've discovered that when reading and writing are personal, students invest themselves in learning. The knowledge they gain moves them forward—they look for more knowledge. Students begin their inquiry about what is important and relevant to them. Each successful and meaningful engagement with reading extends an invitation to write. Students make meaning out of what they read by writing. The more they inquire, the more reading and writing they do.

Making the Changes

My seventh- and eighth-grade special education students have had at least eight years of schooling. Their previous teachers supposedly did all the right things—drill and practice, phonics, how to use context clues, worksheets, lots of workbooks with every reading skill anyone could think of—but still my students had great difficulty. In fact, most of them could not read at a third-grade level. What had been happening to these students all those years? When I decided to change my teaching practices, I did not feel I had anything to lose.

I started making changes in fall 1994, as I learned about the HT process. It was absolutely excruciating to give up the power of being *the* teacher. I was used to being in control; that's what I'd done for sixteen years. One thing I had always told students about behavior management was that democracy ended at the door. Now I saw that this applied not only to my classroom management but to my teaching. For most of my teaching career, I had made all the decisions about what the students read, wrote, and learned from their reading and writing. I tested them on all the genres of reading and mechanics of writing. I gave teacher talks to my students, drilled them on my questions, and lectured them about what to read and write, what to see and appreciate in literature. But even with all of this, I didn't see as much improvement as I thought I would.

Working with Ho'olai one-on-one with the HT process, I was able to see her as a reader and as a writer. Now, I wanted to see my seventh- and eighth-grade students as individual readers and writers with their own strategies, questions, and styles. Like Ho'olai, they brought with them a range of prior knowledge and experiences with texts—some positive, some negative. I wanted them to be able to teach me what they knew, how they came to know what they knew, and to show me where they were going with their knowledge.

My new classroom practices evolved slowly. First, I gave up control. Panic-stricken, I cleaned out my file cabinets and shelves. I got rid of basals and worksheets and workbooks. Then I put myself in the same place as my students: I became a learner in my classroom. I changed my job description from dictator of the language arts to learner of reading and writing. I took it one day at a time and trusted my students to show me what we could learn together.

I started with picture books. Picture books are unheard of in middle school, so this was a great risk for me. Still, I began to read these books to my students. To my surprise, they loved this! I started collecting books by my favorite authors and they loved those too. We studied how these authors wrote and what made these books enjoyable. I was surprised that students became really attached to particular authors. Groups formed on their own. (This was unheard of: *I* formed groups; groups did *not* form by themselves. What was going on?)

Students Taking Charge

I watched carefully and began to see students moving themselves around to people who had the same interests. I thought that these changes were temporary. They weren't. Days passed, and students were still regrouping themselves around another author or theme. Slowly these groups changed. Groups began asking questions about similar topics by different authors, branching out to related topics, and asking about books with more words and on similar topics. Then the biggest change came: students began studying totally unrelated topics, themes, issues, and questions with partners, in groups, or on their own.

In their groups, students created graphic organizers, time lines, charts, and graphs to help them with the information. I began to bring out resource books to help them with their inquiries. I was very surprised when they began to use these books to help them with their projects. They used me as a resource, too. If we did not have enough resources, or the right ones, in the classroom, the students went elsewhere, always coming back with something to help them.

At times, I felt left out of the process, but I was determined to watch and see what my students would do. I was losing control. It was not easy to accept and "stay out" of their learning; my students were learning in spite of me. Sometimes, though, when groups became stalled with their questioning, I would give a mini-lesson to the whole class. Then I noticed that everyone took notes and asked thoughtful, purposeful questions—this had not happened before!

Jerome Harste visited and called what was happening in my classroom *inquiry*. I added this new word to my vocabulary. For me, coming to understand inquiry was a slow and painful process. I noticed impatience creeping into my demeanor. What was the problem? Too few books were being read. I usually demanded that we read one book every two weeks. Some groups had read only two books in nine to ten weeks, far too few books! Some students weren't reading even one complete book. How could they participate in their group projects? I watched.

The students were reading to each other. The better readers were reading to other students. There were usually multiple copies of each title so they could read to each other. (I used to call this cheating!) I saw that even though some students couldn't read the text, they could process and understand the information, the story. They could participate well in the group projects and be a part of the learning process without having to struggle over every single word and sentence. Kids who didn't or couldn't do their reading homework sat and listened carefully while their group members discussed their reading. They even took notes. The groups seemed far more productive than before. I saw a change of attitude toward learning, a willingness to figure out strategies to learn words never before attempted, and the building of a knowledge base. None of this could have happened, or did happen, with my previous style of teaching.

Writing was the next change. In the past, I dictated what the writing assignments were; I had convinced myself that this was the way to teach writing. My students now showed me that I hadn't been teaching them as writers. I watched as they began to use writing to make sense of their reading and to write their reflections. They no longer wrote boring summaries of what they read (plagiarized from the books) or comments to please me; instead, they wrote insightful comments about story parts, personal connections to similar experiences, explosions of personal opinions, or seemingly disconnected comments that were triggered by what was read. This was more than I could handle. What was I supposed to do with this stuff? I did nothing.

Students kept reading and writing, trying to make sense out of what they were reading. They made the transition from picture books to juvenile books to young adult books. Many of the young adult books were ones they never would have attempted before. I tried to help by reading aloud to them books I thought would interest them and would give them different experiences with a variety of genres. I gave lots of book talks on topics they were interested in. I often just sat with them and offered tidbits of information which I thought might help them with their inquiries.

I was very interested in why my students would now attempt books "too difficult" for them—before they complained that everything was too difficult! By listening and participating in their conversations, I found that they discovered they were able to make sense out of picture books. They decided to do the same thing with juvenile and young adult books. They looked at the whole book and figured out what the story was saying. They read the book as best they could, tried to make sense out of what they read, and then asked questions and researched what they didn't understand—just what we do as adult readers. My students discovered this on their own; I didn't teach this directly, but I think I showed them how to do it by doing it myself.

It had been the same with Ho'olai. She brought books and so did I. She shared her books, then I shared mine. Our conversations would initially be about the pictures, then the text, and then we would often drift onto other subjects which would then lead us to new topics, titles of books, and different authors. In the next session, Ho'olai would explore these new topics, books, and authors.

For ten years, I had been administering the Metropolitan Achievement Test as a pre- and post-test. My students' vocabulary scores usually increased by one to two years, but their comprehension scores increased by less than six months. I could not figure out why this was happening. I worked with several different professors, all of whom told me that I must be directly teaching vocabulary. I insisted I was teaching comprehension.

No one was able to help me figure this out. Then I started to work with Ho'olai, and Diane Stephens and all the authors I read while first working with the HT process: Frank Smith (1985, 1988), Judith Newman (1991), Karen Smith (personal communications, 1996), Lucy McCormick Calkins (1986, 1991), Donald Graves (1994). I began to change my thinking about how reading and writing are taught and learned. Changing my thinking, I changed my practices. Now, my students' comprehension scores also go up considerably.

"I have a new theory" (Peterson, 1992) about teaching and learning. I believe that my job is to guide my students beyond what they can already do. I discovered that learning someone else's curriculum (mine) is often meaningless to students. Nothing much is remembered or used. My students need to read for their own purposes and write in their own voices and answer their own questions, not mine. Students need to discover how powerful their own voices can be. I've given back a lot of the responsibility for teaching to them. They choose what they write, read, and what they need to work on. This "new way" of teaching leads us all to learning.

References

Calkins, L. M. (1986). *The art of teaching writing*. Portsmouth, NH: Heinemann.

Calkins, L. M. (1991). *Living between the lines*. Portsmouth, NH: Heinemann.

Graves, D. (1994). *A fresh look at writing*. Portsmouth, NH: Heinemann.

Halliday, M. A. K. (1973). Three aspects of children's language development: Learning language, learning through language, learning about language. In Y. Goodman, M. H. Haussler, & D. Strickland (Eds.), *Oral and written language development research: Impact on the schools*. Urbana, IL: National Council of Teachers of English.

Newman, J. (1991). *Interwoven conversations: Learning and teaching through critical reflection*. Toronto, Ontario: Ontario Institute for Studies in Education.

Peterson, R. (1992). *Life in a crowded place: Making a learning community*. Portsmouth, NH: Heinemann.

Smith, F. (1985). *Reading without nonsense*. New York: Teachers College Press.

Smith, F. (1988). *Understanding reading: A psycholinguistic analysis of reading and learning to read*. Hillsdale, NJ: Erlbaum.

Stephens, D. (Ed.). (1990). *What matters? A primer for teaching reading*. Portsmouth, NH: Heinemann.

HT as Catalyst

Paula Matsunaga
Kapolei Elementary School, Hawaii

Shares how author's reflections on HT as inquiry transformed her approach to first-grade curriculum.

I learned about Hypothesis-Test as part of a graduate class that Diane Stephens taught in fall 1994. At the start of that course, Diane told us there were no required readings or papers. All we needed to do was meet with our child twice a week and complete HT sheets for each of those sessions. She also recommended that we submit a journal which would be a written conversation between us and her. She would read through our documents and respond to them on a weekly basis.

As the semester progressed, we all came to realize that while yes, all we *had* to do was meet with our child and complete the HT sheets, the amount of tension and dissonance that these one-on-one sessions created led us to choose to do much more than we had to. The more I thought I knew about my child, the more questions Diane would ask, and the more I realized I did not know about my child. Diane's questions, and my doubts, provided me with the motivation to do more professional reading about reading, writing, spelling, and other elements involved with emerging literacy. The drive to get these readings done before the next session was insatiable. I wanted to know more so that I could do more for my struggling student.

At the end of the class, as I reflected upon the intense and arduous process that I had just undergone, I realized that I had learned more in one semester than I had ever learned before. I realized that I had given up on sleep and other social activities in pursuit of answers—answers for my own questions and tensions. The motivation was there because I was interested in learning, and more important, because I was answering my own questions.

Incredibly, I found that the tensions never ceased; answers were always accompanied by new questions. Fresh queries grew out of the HT process because HT pushed me to be more holistic. It forced me to look beyond the superficial elements and encouraged me to consider all possible factors. HT put me in a situation similar to a doctor or therapist who is confronted with a new patient.

This was learning! I began to think about how I could take the continuous improvement process that I had just gone through, break it down for my children, and implement it in the classroom. I wanted them to feel the excitement that came from hard work, reflection, and, ultimately, from making connections. I wanted them to experience what true motivation and personal involvement felt like.

Prior to all of this, I had taught what Kathy Short and her colleagues called thematic units (Short, et al. 1996). I chose topics that would be of interest to the children, webbed out integrated activities that included all the content areas and, during the course of the study, brought in activities and experiments to support the children's emerging interests. I struggled to maintain the momentum, working day after day to try to provide new activities and experiments that would answer the questions the children brought up during class. Fatigue and illness brought on by this impossible pace forced me to step back and reflect on my classroom practices. It was then I realized that I was doing all of the work. Yes, I was providing my students with a means to learn content, but I was negating the most important learning. By preparing and predetermining everything, I was not exposing them to the process of answering their own questions. No wonder there was no excitement—I had taken all the joy out of their learning. There were no new discoveries for the children, because there was no empowerment and collaboration. The studies we did revolved around my plans, and I was instinctively working from what I knew. We were not inquiring into the unknown; we were not sharing in the process.

As I thought about HT and the process that I had used to better understand that student both as a reader and a writer, I realized that I had worked from what I saw and knew (made observations), generated interpretations (explored meaning through reflection and countless revisions), and proposed hypotheses and appropriate curricular decisions (developed invitations to further inquiries). These correlated almost perfectly to the curricular framework used by Harste, Short, and Burke (1988) for their authoring cycle in *Creating Classrooms for Authors: The Reading–Writing Connection*. I was excited when I saw that it was possible for me to take the HT process and transfer it into classroom practice. The HT process could become a learning tool for my children. It could help them construct their own knowledge and understandings.

Naming What I Knew

Just as I was struggling with all of this, Jerome Harste was on sabbatical in Hawaii and began coming to one of the graduate classes I was taking. His discussions with our group enabled me to begin naming what I was struggling with. He called the continuous improvement process *inquiry* and argued that education is inquiry and that the personal and collective questions of learners ought to be the heart of curriculum (personal communications with Harste, 1995; also see Short & Harste with Burke, 1996).

So now what? I agreed with it all implicitly, but I couldn't state it explicitly. More important, I didn't know where or how to begin. I did not see how all of this theory was applicable to a classroom for six-year-olds. My internal tensions drove me to read more. *Learning Together through Inquiry* (Short et al., 1996) enabled me to see that I did not have to throw out what I was doing, I just needed to adjust and modify my focus. They used many of the same materials, activities, and books to contrast inquiry and thematic units. This helped me to see that a curriculum based on student-generated questions was possible for emerging readers and writers. I realized that the road block was mine. I had been accepting approximations during our readers' and writers' workshops, but for some reason, I had not felt that approximations were appropriate during our content studies. For example, I allowed invented spellings and echo reading, but if a child mislabeled a sketch or drawing, I would not allow that. Once I saw this, I was able to continue on with more confidence and enthusiasm.

The following summer, I took a weeklong summer class from Karen Smith, then an associate executive director of the National Council of Teachers of English. With Karen's help and handouts (personal communications, 1996), I began my move from thematic units toward an inquiry-based curriculum. I now had some goals to work toward and ideas to play with. I knew, however, that I needed to hold onto the theory, the essence of inquiry, and use it to establish the appropriate environment in my classroom. Simultaneously, I needed to provide the necessary structure and scaffolding for each and every child. I needed to consider the varying levels of self-confidence, independence, and experience (with the world and with the inquiry process), and the amount and quality of support that each child would or would not receive at home.

Moving toward Inquiry

I entered the new school year excited and ready to make the leap from thematic units to an inquiry-based curriculum. I realized that I would be learning as I was going, but I just could not see any other way to do it. I began by asking my students, "What do good researchers do?" Building a web together, we defined a researcher as someone who solves problems and answers their own questions. I wanted to keep this initial web as baseline data and then add to it as the year went on. When I asked them how researchers got their answers, the children's only response—look in books—helped me understand that I would need to help them develop other ways of answering questions.

For our first attempt at inquiry, I chose to play it safe. Our first-grade curriculum starts with a look at "Me and Who I Am with My Family and My Community." For about two weeks, I used some of the activities from my thematic unit file to provide some background knowledge for the children. We did "Me Webs," family interviews, and sense walks. As Karen Smith had recommended, taking time at the beginning to learn to explore our subject paid dividends. The class webs we subsequently did about what we knew and wanted to learn about ourselves were stronger than any we had done before. The class came up with things like, "I am a son or a daughter." "I am a student in school." "I have five senses." The language was self-generated and I did not have to lead or pull for these responses. But what amazed me most were the questions the children came up with for what they wanted to learn. For example, "We need to learn to read and write." "Why?" "We're making books." "Why don't our books look like library books?" These questions helped the inquiry process fall into place. After we got the questions, the class decided to interview adults (parents, principal, vice principal, counselor, and so on) to determine why we need to learn to read and write, and they decided to take some learning trips to printing places to see why our published books did not look like library books.

These student-centered activities were self-motivated ones. The children did the work and kept themselves excited and tenaciously driven. This allowed me to truly be a facilitator and observer. For instance, I suggested that we web and graph the reasons why we need to learn to read and write. The children asked, "Why should we do that?" I responded, "So that we can see our data more clearly." The class agreed and we spent the afternoon webbing and graphing the information that we had collected.

A similar experience occurred when I suggested that we do a Venn diagram for the similarities and differences between a self-published and printed book. My explanation to the class centered around the ability of the Venn diagram to help us see things more clearly. This set of questions brought up a new set, and we embarked on the inquiry cycle all over again. This time the children's questions took us in the direction of papermaking, trees, conservation, and recycling. As a direct result of this inquiry, the children understood that they had a direct responsibility and choice to conserve paper, protect trees, and recycle materials in order to help protect our planet. I have no doubt that an inquiry approach would have been just as powerful for older, more experienced children.

Through the inquiry process, the children also started to see the significance of "basic skills." As one of the tangents to our study, we diagramed a web that showed reasons why we write. The children came up with things such as "to share what we know," "to help us remember things," "to let us teach someone something," "to help us see what we already know." I asked them why this was important. Their response made public the fundamental reason for writing: writing, the children said, helps us to communicate. This child-driven conclusion brought a new tone to our writers' workshop. The children came to realize that this time was important because it would help them to become better writers. As they began to take more risks and apply what they learned or observed in their writing, spelling charts and the studying of good writers took on new meaning.

As we continued along our journey, we also flow-charted what we had been doing. This allowed me to help the children become metacognitively aware of the inquiry process, and also provided me with a critical assessment of what they knew and how they felt about inquiry. As a part of this awareness, I taught the children life skills, such as graphing, how to set up an interview, and how to interview people in a meaningful context. Their questions and action plans provided me with significant moments to teach the skillfulness of inquiry. More important, the children were witnessing how these tools or skills could help them to learn. Through this hands-on process, they were beginning to realize why it was important to learn these tools or skills.

Curriculum planning became a *daily* after-school activity for me. Before moving to an inquiry-based approach, I had been able to plan at least two to three days in advance, but now that I knew what learning was about, I could no longer do that. I could not plan for the next day without reflecting on what had happened that day. It was extremely stressful at times, but I loved it. The children were working from their interests or tensions and developing action plans for their questions. I was enabling them to work through their problems, just as Diane had helped me to work through my professional questions in her graduate course. Carol Avery said it best in her book, . . . *And with a Light Touch* (1993), "The heart and art of teaching is applying, reflecting, and revising one's evolving beliefs in the context of day-to-day developments in the classroom" (p. 87).

New Insights

At the end of every school year, I send home an end-of-year evaluation for my parents to complete. Many expressed how they enjoyed the inquiry projects and how they had fun working on them with their children. Some of their comments helped me understand how much the children had internalized. One parent wrote:

> My child knew exactly how he wanted to answer his football question. All I had to do was take him to the library, help him find the football books, and assist him with parts of the reading. He was interested, motivated, and very self-driven. I couldn't believe it, but he knew what he wanted to do and how he was going to do it.

Another parent responded:

> I didn't know that my daughter could solve her own problems. After all, she's only six years old. But the other day, she wanted to buy something. She counted her money and knew that she didn't have enough. She came to me and said, "Mom, I need 60 cents more to buy my notebook, my plan is to do more jobs. Can I do that?"

Another parent wrote:

> My son came home after doing his first presentation and told me that he didn't talk loud enough, but he knows what to work on to be better. The next time, he practiced and he came home feeling very proud of himself. He knew that he had improved.

Another student had wanted to learn more about dolphins for his individual inquiry project. With the help of his mother, who had prior experience as a dolphin trainer, Tyrell went out, learned more, and came back to class with a poster as a way of sharing what he had learned. About two weeks after his presentation, he stumbled upon a dolphin book in our class library. Scanning the pictures, he realized that there was a section that helped him to answer a few other questions he and his mom had been dealing with at home, beyond the presentation. He came up to me and asked, "Can I copy this down, so that I can take it home to discuss it with Mom?" I simply replied, "What do you think?" He set about to copy it. Mom wrote back the next day:

> I can't believe he found this on his own. I don't think that he can even read what the book said. I will certainly try to save money to make sure that I can take him to the Dolphin University at Sea Life Park, so that he can see for himself what we have been reading and writing about.

My experiences with six-year-olds has shown me how a student-driven inquiry project can bring meaning to the other components of our curriculum, such as our writers' workshop. It has also proven to me that young children can learn and can use broad, universal or umbrella concepts (Short, Schroeder et al., 1996) as curriculum organizers. An inquiry-based curriculum provides children with the environment and opportunities to investigate their own questions, tensions, and dissonances and learn to understand concepts like interdependence (personal communications with J. Hayashi, 1997), discovery, harmony, and change (Short, Schroeder et al., 1996). These concepts help children see where they fit in a larger system (their community, state, or world). They grow to understand the relationship between these concepts and the survival of life and the sustenance of our planet.

Inquiry can become the intangible link between theory, classroom practice, and our world. An inquiry-based curriculum helps children develop the characteristics and skills that we deem important for our students. We all learn by trial and error and "practice makes perfect"; therefore, if we want our children to be critical thinkers and problem solvers, we need to provide them with the opportunities to do these things in the classroom. An inquiry-based curriculum allows us to do this. It also helps children understand the joy of learning that comes from making connections and seeing relationships. It gives them the inquiry process as a tool for problem solving and personal or self-improvement, which is something that they can take with them and use as they continue to grow as learners. It enables them to develop the skills, qualities, and attitudes that our state and national standards, and ultimately the economic and business sectors, are calling for in our graduates.

I have worked through the inquiry process. I have seen for myself how powerful a tool it can be both for my children and me. I now see why Harste says that education is inquiry and inquiry is education (personal communications with Harste, 1995; see also Short & Harste with Burke, 1996). The inquiry process aids in continuous improvement or learning for both children and adults. Inquiry, like HT, is not just a matter of curriculum problem solving, it is a style of living. It empowers individuals to see that they can make a difference in current situations with what they have learned, and it encourages them to share what they have learned with others.

References

Avery, C. (1993). . . . *And with a light touch: Learning about reading, writing, and teaching with first graders.* Portsmouth, NH: Heinemann.

Harste, J. C., & Short, K., with Burke, C. (1988). *Creating classrooms for authors: The reading–writing connection.* Portsmouth, NH: Heinemann.

Short, K., & Harste, J. C., with Burke, C. (1996). *Creating classrooms for authors and inquirers.* Portsmouth, NH: Heinemann.

Short, K., Schroeder, J., Laird, J., Kauffman, G., Ferguson, M. J., & Crawford, K. (1996). *Learning together through inquiry: From Columbus to integrated curriculum.* York, ME: Stenhouse.

Afterword

Diane Stephens and Jennifer Story

This book was written to help teachers better understand the HT process. As we hope the reader now understands, HT is a way of thinking, and the teachers who wrote chapters for this book learned HT as a way of thinking about a child they worried about as a reader. The process itself looks more straightforward than it sometimes plays out: Teachers record observations, brainstorm at least five possible interpretations, look across all interpretations (e.g., if there were ten observations, there would be fifty interpretations), and construct one to three hypotheses they want to test about the child as reader and learner. Teachers then make curricular decisions—plans for learning more about the child by testing out their hypotheses. The cycle then repeats as observations are made based on the child's responses to the curricular invitations. Once teachers have tested a number of hypotheses, they become "pretty sure" about their child as reader and learner and begin to make instructional plans to support the child, building on what they understand about that child.

Each of these "parts" takes a while to master. Too often, teachers at first write down judgments about what they noticed, rather than *what* they noticed. Then it is often hard to generate at least five interpretations. Teachers often realize they need to understand more about the reading/learning process in order to do so. When first constructing hypotheses, teachers often "move over" an interpretation which was their initial judgment, rather than looking across all interpretations and trying to come up with a pattern that might explain the diverse observations. Lastly, it takes a while for teachers to feel comfortable using curricular decisions not to try to "fix" what they nearly instantaneously thought was broken, but rather to use curricular decisions to test out hypotheses.

As teachers, we rely on our learned ability to make quick decisions. HT asks us to slow down the process, to spend perhaps a month or six weeks just getting to know a child as reader and learner before deciding how best to help the child progress in those areas. This "slowing down" is uncomfortable and violates our tendency to want to "fix" children as soon as possible. But the HT process is not designed as a "quick fix." It is instead a way to carefully, deeply, and thoughtfully get to know a child who is struggling, so that any planned intervention or instructional act will indeed prove useful for that child. The child studied via HT is usually a child for whom previous well-intended "quick fixes" have not worked. HT is about understanding—deeply, thoroughly—so that our actions as teachers can truly make a difference in the life of a child.

In this book, we have tried to explain that process, in the abstract as well as in the particular. We wanted to show you the HT process as it played out for teachers who were learning it and for the children with whom they learned. Susan Oka-Yamashita, Lynn Yoshizaki, Elaine Tsuchiyama, and Diane Parker detail their learning process for us as they simultaneously detail what and how they learned about a child with whom they worked. We also wanted to help readers understand that because the HT process is a way of thinking, its usefulness often goes beyond the one-on-one setting and becomes a means for making connections to other aspects of curriculum as well as to whole-class settings. Paula Matsunaga therefore shows how her experience as an HT learner caused her to examine the learning process she was providing to her first graders. Bette Ito explains how her HT work with a first grader led to major changes in her instructional practices with seventh and eighth graders. Sandie Kubota shows how she used HT to help one child in her first/second-grade classroom, while Jennifer Story reveals how she uses the HT process for her entire class.

Our emphasis in this was on explaining the HT process, showing how it was learned via case studies and revealing some of the "next steps" taken by teachers who initially learned the process in one-on-one settings. We told our story because readers who had responded both to our initial article about HT (in *Language Arts,* 1996) and our issue of *Primary Voices K–6* (January 1997) wanted more detail, more examples, closer looks at students, closer looks at teachers. Reviewers of this book (in manuscript form) feel readers have an opportunity to learn the HT process alongside the teachers who authored this text. But another request has been made: How is it, we have been asked, that the HT process is taught? What happens in the "classrooms" in which teachers learn how to "do" the HT process? What goes on in the mind of the teacher of teachers as she or he makes plans to introduce teachers to a way of thinking they are asked to "try on"?

In response to this request, a companion volume, *Teaching the HT Process,* is in process. Meanwhile, any of you wishing to understand more about the process of teaching and learning HT can contact the authors of this volume. Each of us will help in any way that we can. Our e-mail addresses (as of Fall 1999) are listed with the personal profiles at the end of the book.

We've all tried on HT as a way of thinking and found that, by broadening and deepening our understanding of children as readers, we've been able to make a difference in the life of a child. We've been able to change patterns. Our second greatest joy is to help others do the same.

Editors

Jennifer Story is a sixth-grade teacher at Dole Middle School in Honolulu, Hawaii, and a doctoral student at the University of Hawaii. For the past six years, she has served as co-editor of *Primary Voices K–6.* Jennifer has been using the HT process since 1986, when she was working on her M.Ed. at the University of North Carolina–Wilmington.
E-mail Address: story@hawaii.edu

Diane Stephens prepared this book while she was a professor at the University of Hawaii–Manoa. Now she is at the University of South Carolina. She is co-author of *Looking Closely,* also published by NCTE, and editor of *What Matters: A Primer for Teaching Reading.* For the past seven years, she has served as co-editor of *Primary Voices K–6,* an NCTE journal by and for teachers. Diane and her colleagues have also written about the HT process in an article for *Language Arts* (February 1996) and an issue of *Primary Voices* (January 1997).
E-mail Address: stephensd@gwm.sc.edu

Note: E-mail addresses were current as of Fall 1999.

Contributors

Bette Jane Ito is a teacher at Wahiawa Middle School in Wahiawa, Hawaii. She teaches English and reading to sixth, seventh, and eighth graders. For the past six years, she has been researching and using critical inquiry and the HT process in her teaching practice.
E-mail Address: itob001@hawaii.rr.com

Sandie Kubota has been teaching in Hawaii for seventeen years. She has worked with children with special needs, as lead teacher for a Title 1 program, and currently teaches in a looping situation with grades 1 and 2, all in the Central Oahu District. She also works with University of Hawaii students. She is a member of Pi Lambda Theta, a professional organization for educators. She has published an article on the HT process in *Primary Voices K–6.* Her current professional interests are in the areas of reading, writing, and assessment.
E-mail Address: sumi@hawaii.rr.com

Paula Matsunaga is a first-grade teacher at Kapolei Elementary School on the island of Oahu. She previously served as the school's curriculum coordinator and has worked as a Reading Recovery teacher. While a master's degree student of Diane Stephens, Paula explored the concept of inquiry in her thesis. Presently her research interests include exploring literacy and utilizing the inquiry cycle as a curricular framework.
E-mail Address: paula_matsunaga@notes.k12.hi.us

Susan Oka-Yamashita is now a third-grade teacher at Mililani Waena Elementary School. She met Diane Stephens through the university classes held for teachers in Oahu's Central District while working at Wahiawa Elementary School. This has taken her on an incredible journey into learning, which helped her receive her master's degree in elementary education in December 1996.
E-mail Address: okayamas@hawaii.edu

Diane Parker has taught in Connecticut and Hawaii, and is currently a primary grade teacher at Waikele Elementary School in the Hawaii public school system and a mentor teacher and lecturer in the University of Hawaii preservice teacher education program. As a teacher–researcher, she is deeply committed to her own learning as well as to that of her students; she is interested in many issues related to curriculum, assessment, and teacher education. She shares her classroom stories with other teachers at conferences and through her

Note: E-mail addresses were current as of Fall 1999.

writings, which include *Jamie: A Literacy Story*, and several articles published in educational journals.
E-mail Address: dparker@hawaii.edu *or* diane_parker@notes.k12.hi.us

Elaine Tsuchiyama has taught for twenty-nine years in Hawaii's public school system. Her experiences have ranged from teaching reading through a schoolwide basal text to an open classroom format called a modified three-on-two (two teachers and an educational aide with two grade levels). Teaching assignments included combination kindergarten/ first grade and first/second grade, self-contained first and sixth grades, and a gifted/talented program which included students from the first through sixth grade. Elaine spent two years as teacher liaison with the University of Hawaii's "Philosophy in the Schools" project. She completed her master's degree in education at the University of Hawaii in 1999.

Lynn Yoshizaki resides in Wahiawa, Hawaii. She has been in the public school system for twenty-nine years. From the beginning of her career, she questioned the nature of teaching and learning. She constantly sought the "beneath the surface" understanding of her query. Her thirst to internalize this art of real teaching led her to participate in the "Engagements" project with Diane Stephens. This experience was most revealing and rejuvenating to her growth as a teacher. Lynn now serves as Title 1 lead teacher at Wahiawa Elementary School.
E-mail Address: lyyoshiz@makani.K12.hi.us

Note: E-mail addresses were current as of Fall 1999.

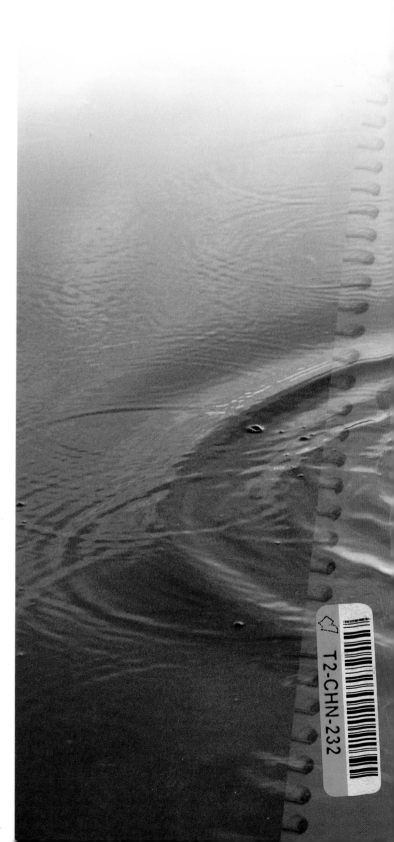

Diane Stephens and Jennifer Story have produced a tour de force with *Assessment as Inquiry: Learning the Hypothesis-Test Process*. Their work describes a different way of thinking, of looking at one's teaching and students' learning as a recursive process of Hypothesizing and Testing. Included in the book are stories from classroom teachers learning the process and implementing it in their classrooms with individual students. English language arts teachers looking for authentic assessment techniques will find here a way to interweave teaching and assessment. The HT process provides tools for continuous observation of students, determining first and foremost what each student needs to succeed in the classroom.

National Council of Teachers of English
1111 W. Kenyon Road, Urbana, Illinois 61801-1096
1-800-369-6283 or 217-328-3870
www.ncte.org

ISBN 0-8141-2785-1

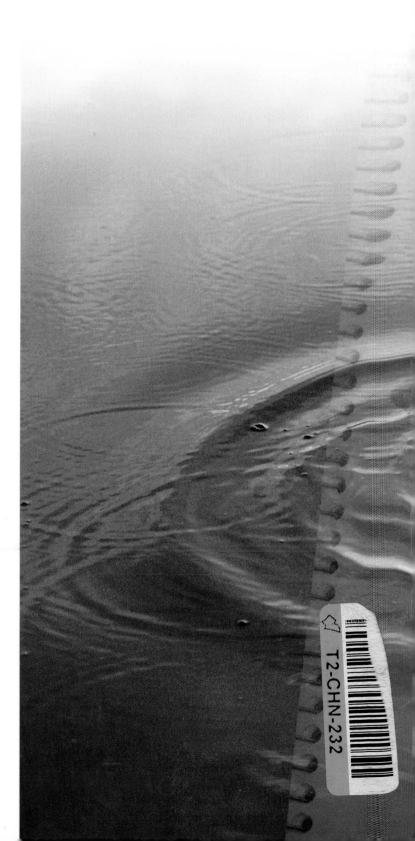

Diane Stephens and Jennifer Story have produced a tour de force with *Assessment as Inquiry: Learning the Hypothesis-Test Process.* Their work describes a different way of thinking, of looking at one's teaching and students' learning as a recursive process of Hypothesizing and Testing. Included in the book are stories from classroom teachers learning the process and implementing it in their classrooms with individual students. English language arts teachers looking for authentic assessment techniques will find here a way to interweave teaching and assessment. The HT process provides tools for continuous observation of students, determining first and foremost what each student needs to succeed in the classroom.

National Council of Teachers of English
1111 W. Kenyon Road, Urbana, Illinois 61801-1096
1-800-369-6283 or 217-328-3870
www.ncte.org

ISBN 0-8141-2785-1

9 780814 127858

90000